Praise for
The Chocolate Conversation and Rose Fass

"Rose Fass is the undisputed master of organizational dynamics, and this book proves she has the bead on what it takes to transform companies and brands in these challenging times. The simplicity of her idea—that everything that matters happens 'in the conversation'—is both essential and critical for success in a complex world. Read the book, join the conversation, and bask in Rose's wisdom, as I've done many times in my career."
— Bob Greenberg, founder, chairman and CEO, R/GA

"My senior leadership team was formed through acquisitions, restructuring, and a compelling need to reinvent our business. We had a clear mission, or so we thought. Instead our team was fragmented and we needed help. In walks a dynamic, insightful woman asking us to define *chocolate*?! It triggered a conversation that led us to recognize that past victories would not take us into the future—and to instead frame a unified strategy and focused actions. We got the job done. When I assumed my next executive leadership role, the first call I made was to that same dynamic woman, Rose Fass, for my next 'chocolate conversation.'"
— Karen T. Cone, general manager,
Worldwide Financial Services, Microsoft

"Rose Fass is a skilled practitioner of the thoughts, ideas, and concepts she writes about in this outstanding book. *The Chocolate Conversation* is not a pie in the sky reading. Her conversations with you throughout these pages are full of rich insight that will strip away the fluff and demonstrate that meaningful organizational change is rooted in multi-level, cross-functional conversations. Rose's book underscores the old maxim: if you don't like change, you are going to like irrelevancy even less."
— Thomas A. Kayser, author of
Mining Group Gold and *Building Team Power*

"*The Chocolate Conversation* is a must-read and field manual for anyone setting out to change their company from the heart and hand of the master change maker herself, Rose Fass. Rose's warmth and wit, down-to-earth style, and galvanizing authority is on every page. "Run, don't walk, to get your copy of this delightful and wildly informative book."

— Kevin Allen, founder and CEO, re:kap, and author of the *WSJ* best-seller *The Hidden Agenda: A Proven Way to Win Business and Create a Following*

"Rose Fass has written a remarkably rich book that carries the reader along swiftly, easily, and enjoyably from cover to cover. Rose shows her experienced judgment on how to reframe thinking and conversations, and incites her readers to take action."

— Peter Koestenbaum, PhD, founder and chairman of PiB and the Koestenbaum Institute

"True brilliance is not about developing complex theories or pontificating about piles of research reporting out on what has already happened. True brilliance is about simplifying complex issues and harnessing people's energy to change the world. In that light, *The Chocolate Conversion* is simply brilliant. Rose brings her experience, inherent intellect, and frankly raw talent forward in to this book. She is a strategist, motivator, and business leader. She brings clarity to chaos, finds solutions to big business problems, and most importantly drives and delivers results. Putting the tools delivered in this book into action will be the single most important business investment you can make in the coming years."

— Martha Delehanty, SVP, Human Resources, Verizon Enterprise Solutions

"I know Rose and, boy, do I know chocolate. Together they hold a conversation that will change you and your company. In today's world, laden with so many know-it-all books full of the same old promises, Rose Fass' insights beg us to have a dialogue that reframes our thinking and 'talk time' to get people to act."

— Albert Gaulden, founding director, The Sedona Intensive™ and author of *You're Not Who You Think You Are*

rose fass

the chocolate conversation

Lead Bittersweet Change, Transform Your Business

bibliomotion
books + media

First published by Bibliomotion, Inc.

33 Manchester Road
Brookline, MA 02446
Tel: 617-934-2427
www.bibliomotion.com

Printed in the United States of America

Library of Congress Cataloging-in-Publication Data

Fass, Rose.
    The chocolate conversation : lead bittersweet change, transform your business / by Rose Fass.
        pages cm
    Includes bibliographical references and index.
    ISBN 978-1-937134-49-5 (hardcover : alk. paper) —
ISBN 978-1-937134-50-1 (ebook) — ISBN 978-1-937134-51-8 (enhanced ebook)
    1. Organizational change. 2. Leadership. I. Title.
    HD58.8.F369 2013
    658.4'063—dc23
                        2012050427

For my Dad,
Peter Angelo Mazza
June 6, 1923–August 18, 2012

Contents

Foreword

by Bill McDermott

Throughout my career, I tend to adopt wisdom from others very cautiously. Too many "thought leaders" offer clever but unproven advice. Rose Fass, however, is a precious exception, with guidance that comes from a career's worth of success.

Rose and I first worked together when she participated in hiring me at Xerox, where she established herself as a mentor and a trusted counselor to many leaders, and positively influenced many lives, including my own. Seventeen years after we first met, I hired her to join me at Gartner. A strategic thinker with a rare gift for bringing structure to chaos, Rose has consistently helped teams overcome their differences and collaborate to achieve amazing things. Her secret, which she reveals in *The Chocolate Conversation*, brings to mind something Henry Kissinger once told me, advice I have never forgotten: "Whatever must be done eventually should be done immediately." Rose understands something too many leaders easily forget, that big, bold change happens one conversation at a time, but without urgency and clarity, those critical conversations fall flat, and the whole organization suffers.

Rose's message is critical for these times. As the consumer revolution and rapid innovations in technology continue to disrupt entire industries, enterprises from New York to New Delhi are realizing that constant change is a necessity. My advice to them and to you is to read this book. It will help you break through the inevitable chaos and more quickly drive success.

Preface

Over the years, I have been invited to speak to diverse audiences on the subject of leadership and transformation. Following these engagements, I am often asked if I have written a book. For those of you who have resonated with me, your encouragement got me here.

I dedicate this book to my dad, whose leadership, strength, and integrity taught me what it means to go the distance and to stay the course through challenging times. While I was writing this book, my father, a U.S. Marine who served in World War II, a poet, and a business executive, fought his final battle. He died of congestive heart failure on Saturday, August 18, at 3:55 in the afternoon. This book is for you, Dad. Thank you for leading me through life.

I look back on my career now and I see where and how the lessons of my childhood and those of my early career in the corporate world got me to where I am today, talking to you. Some of the most important lessons didn't look like lessons at the time—they just looked like life.

Later in the book, I'll reference my time at Xerox, where I started in sales on a management fast track and eighteen years later became the chief transformation officer. Several years after that, I was recruited by Gartner, a well-regarded IT research firm, to create, staff, and lead a center for business transformation. In 2001, I filed for incorporation of *fassforward*. Up until then, I had always worked for a publicly traded company. This was my first venture into entrepreneurship. I was on my own. It was a scary time for me.

As with many entrepreneurs, I started working from my home. My soon-to-be partner, Gavin McMahon, was in Texas working on getting his United States residency. While he was gone, I secured our first client and found a small office space above the local post office.

The rent was modest and the space was just big enough for two desks and a small conference table. Fortunately, a friend told me about a used office furniture place not far from the post office. The guys there were great, and they sold me furniture at a reasonable price and threw in a wall-mounted whiteboard. My husband brought in a painter who plastered and painted the walls. I put a chair rail around the perimeter of the office to give it some dimension and I had two phones and two desktop computers installed. When Gavin returned from Texas, we were set up and ready to go.

My new client phoned and asked if I could meet with the company's head of research and development, who was coming in from Canada. My client wanted to meet in our office. This was in the days following 9/11, when midtown office space for everyone was tight—many companies had to squeeze into their midtown offices because they no longer had access to their downtown spaces.

I wasn't thrilled about having them come to the post office, but what could I do?

That evening, I went to the store and bought cleaning supplies to wash down the walls of the elevator. Once everyone left the building, I changed into my jeans, went down to the lobby, locked the front door, and began cleaning the elevator.

The rug smelled of mildew. I scrubbed and scrubbed, to no avail. Well, mildew smell would not do, so I ripped up the rug, intending to throw it away. That was no easy feat—I broke a few nails in the process.

Hoping no one I knew would be walking by, I dragged the

rug to the front door and peeked out onto the street. Good! The coast was clear! I pulled the rug to the end of the block and dumped it into a large trash can.

After I scrubbed the elevator floor, I laid newspaper down to keep it clean while I started on the walls. As fate would have it, there was a picture of Anne Mulcahy, my former boss at Xerox, looking up at me from the *Wall Street Journal*. Here I was, looking back, rag in one hand, Fantastik cleaner in the other, covered in dirt and with broken nails, cleaning the elevator in the local post office.

The voice in my head went like this: "What is wrong with this picture? What have I done? I used to be a 'big piece of stuff,' and now I'm a 'Gertie Schmertz,' with an office the size of a bookie joint, across from the train tracks." That's when I sat down on the elevator floor and had a meltdown.

With my head in my hands and adrift in all those "woe is me" thoughts, I lost track of the time until I looked up and noticed it was dark outside. And, there, at the front of the building, was my husband, Ron, banging on the door and calling to me through the glass to open up and let him in. I couldn't move. He fumbled for his key and came rushing in.

There I sat, disheveled and unintelligible. I was sobbing and pointing to the picture in the newspaper. Ron connected the dots, grasped the situation—and demanded that I get up.

To know Ron is to understand what happened next. He did not take me into his arms and soothingly tell me it would all be okay. He pulled me to my feet and said, "You are bigger than this. It's not where you work or who you work for that makes you good, it's the work you do and WHO YOU ARE. This place does not define you. YOU do."

I pulled myself together, finished the rest of the cleaning, and went home.

The next day, Gavin met our prospective client in the lobby. I laughed to myself when I heard that he opted to take the stairs.

Once we were seated around the conference table, listening to the client's business challenges and brainstorming ideas, I was in the zone—*my* zone. I didn't need the props to engage in a productive discussion and propose an approach that would work. We got the verbal agreement to put together a statement of work and began the process of helping our client transform his business.

After our client left, I told Gavin about that night in the elevator. It was a turning point in my own transformation. Leaving the life—and the world—around which I'd built my career was bittersweet, but the rewards have been beyond what I could have ever hoped for.

We've grown a business we can both be proud of, and in the process we've grown, too. What I came to realize is that my experience and my skills were still with me. I knew I could call on that talent to help other businesses avoid common pitfalls and embark on a successful transformation.

We did it first at Estée Lauder when we successfully resolved the cultural issues between MAC and Estée Lauder's R&D teams. We followed with the formation of innovation teams at Estée Lauder that crossed businesses and resulted in a record number of new product and packaging patents in the first six months of the project.

Later, we began working with Interpublic Group of Companies, successfully creating a common operational business process across all their agencies. The CEO finally was able to view the financial performance of each agency and the aggregate of the holding company in an accurate and consistent format.

Howard Draft and Laurence Boschetto brought us in on the merger of Draft and FCB, formerly known as Foote, Cone & Belding. Here we were able to work with the leadership of both companies on a soup-to-nuts transformation that took us around the globe over a two-year period. *Ad Age* later referred to the Draftfcb merger as "uncommonly successful" and the only one of its kind.

A colleague who Gavin and I worked with at Gartner was hired by a global credit card company to head up its research group for a newly formed business unit. She introduced us to the president. We were hired by him and, with the president and his senior team, we successfully over a one-year period, helped them transform their business.

fassforward continues today to assist and guide our clients through the bittersweet change of transformation. We've come a long way from the office over the post office and the mildewed rug on the elevator floor.

As for me, I've come a long way, too.

As a young girl, I never thought about being a corporate executive. I loved to read and write poetry. I enjoyed all things creative and artistic.

My dad is the one who taught me how to express my ideas. He gave me a love for poetry and philosophy. My father believed in self-reliance, and so I listened to his lessons on Emerson and Thoreau with rapt attention. I hung on his every word, listening for hours as he recited poetry: Robert Frost's *The Road Not Taken* and Walt Whitman's *Leaves of Grass* were among his favorites. They became mine.

My father went to college in the evenings on the GI Bill and did different jobs during the day. He was articulate, well read, and always dressed in a suit. He would often remind us that our appearance was our introduction to the world. He was ever aware that we were living in an Italian neighborhood. There were all types of families, and many of the parents spoke broken English and their children spoke in slang. Dad insisted we speak properly. He taught us new vocabulary words regularly and encouraged us to use them.

My father taught me many things, but this story is my favorite. It is my signature story:

Walt Disney talent scouts came to Utica, New York. My best friend's cousin, Annette Funicello, was discovered and invited to audition with Walt Disney for a new series, *The Mickey Mouse Club*. Annette was several years older than we were, but, boy, were we jealous!

All of my friends were Italian-American girls, brunettes with big brown eyes, just like me—and just like Annette. We were all cute and we could all dance. So the big question was, "Why her?"

Roseanne, Annette's cousin, tried to explain that Annette had taken dance lessons, was very talented, and had everything they were looking for—but we didn't want to hear it. We hardly knew Annette because she was in junior high and we were in grade school, but we decided we didn't like her. We walked home from school every day saying bad things about her.

I was so depressed to know that a girl from Utica was going to be famous and it wasn't going to be me! I moped for days. I drove my parents crazy.

My mother tried to cheer me up. She told me that we see down the street, but God sees around the corner, and I couldn't know what was waiting for me around that corner. I asked her if she knew. She said, "*Your* time will come, Rose, and when it does, you'll know." My snippy, little grade-school response was, "When? Next Tuesday?" Mom told me to be patient. I was not at all satisfied with her answer, so I continued to mope.

At the end of the week, I was walking home from school commiserating with my friends. When we got to my street, I waved goodbye. I headed toward the house with my head down, still despondent over what was clearly the wrong choice by those Walt Disney people. I was not at all sure that I would survive not being famous.

It was a rare and beautiful spring day. Under normal circumstances, I would have been delighted. Upstate New York winters always seemed endless in their dreariness. Today was a gorgeous exception. My dad was standing in front of our house picking dandelions from a patch of grass we referred to as our front yard.

Head down, I mumbled, "Hello," as I attempted to walk by him. It didn't work. He firmly called to me, "Rose, I want to see you." Having read a little of my dad's story earlier in this preface, you can imagine my "mopy-ness" didn't go over well with my self-reliant, make-your-own-way dad. He loved me dearly but he had no patience for my self-indulgent, celebrity fantasy about being discovered by the Disney scouts—and my devastation that someone else got picked, and "Why not me?"

I knew he wasn't pleased with me, so I tried to postpone the encounter. He was not to be put off, however. He held up a dandelion. He said, "Rose, what do you see?" I was aware that the answer on the tip of my tongue wasn't going to fly, so I shrugged and said, "It's a dandelion, Dad." He came right back at me: "Rose, look deeper, what do you *really* see?" Even at nine, I was the Queen of Rhetorical Responses. I replied, "I don't know, Dad, what do *you* see?" He knew what I was doing, and, a little amused, he humored me.

And, then…he surprised me: "I see the end of a long winter, the dawn of a new season, children frolicking in their front yards, bringing bunches of these dandelions to their mothers to place in juice glasses on the sills of kitchen windows. I see lovers walking hand in hand, stopping to pick bunches of them to exchange in silent I love yous. I see the promise of warm summer days and endless fragrant nights." I could feel my tears and the lump in my throat. All I could say was, "You see a lot, Dad."

He smiled and said, "Soon, Rose, the prettier flowers will come along, and this once welcome introduction to spring will become an intruder—a distortion to the lawn. That's when I, like many homeowners, will go to the local nurseries to buy chemicals to rid our lawns of this weed. But the beauty of the dandelion does not lie in its brief moment of glory. For those of us who have worked at pulling up dandelions, we know they come back each year, double fold. The beauty of the dandelion is, it's in its root and its resilience."

He paused for a moment to let that sink in. Then, he said, *"Your mother and I named you 'Rose,' but roses are fragile. In your heart, you need to be a dandelion."*

I don't know exactly what happened to me, just that some deep understanding gripped my being. I cried while my dad held me.

In the arms of a poet, a philosopher, and a U.S. Marine, I learned my life's most important lesson: resilience. I have carried that story with me ever since. Over the years, friends, students, and colleagues have solicited my perspective on what I consider to be the most significant attribute of well-regarded leaders. There are probably a dozen or more good responses to this question. What *I* would call attention to are those individuals who make a conscious effort to keep the ego in check, those who resist becoming overly inflated in times of triumph or self-flagellating in times of challenge. There is joy during the moments of glory and steadfastness in times of defeat.

The authentic leaders are the ones who keep coming back, the ones who are resilient and focused and who fight to keep their integrity and help others do the same. They are the ones who lead by example, those who go the distance. I refer to them as kindred spirits—they are my fellow dandelions.

Thank you, Dad. In my heart,
I know I am a dandelion—because of you.
Rose Fass, February, 2013

Introduction

The Chocolate Conversation

If you picked up this book because you found the title intriguing, then you're probably asking the question, "What is a Chocolate Conversation and what does that have to do with transforming my company?"

So far, so good. Now you've started a conversation with me—one I really want to have with you. What if I told you that everything regarding your leadership, the market leadership of your company, followership, and change happens in the conversation? What if I went so far as to say that the single factor that determines success or failure is the conversation? Still listening? Okay. Here's how this all got started.

Bring Your Own Chocolate

A few years after I graduated from college, I was invited to a "Death by Chocolate" party. It was a BYOC invitation: "Bring your own chocolate" to share with everyone. What a hoot! I prepared my award-winning, killer chocolate cake, figuring I'd be the hit of the party—and off I went.

I anticipated the usual suspects: chewy double-fudge brownies, chocolate chunk cookies, and chocolate mousse. I'd set my sights too low—when I arrived, there before me was a seven-foot table laden with every conceivable chocolate confection I could imagine: éclairs nestled among soufflés, truffles, hand-dipped fruit—a veritable chocolate lover's paradise. Alas, the only thing missing was the magic potion to make all the calories disappear before the afterglow of the evening appeared on my derriere.

Competition was stiff and the conversations about chocolate were intense: texture, density, aroma, percentage of cacao. These were serious chocolate snobs! One very slim woman declared, "When I indulge, it's got to be high quality—something I can savor long after I've eaten it." The guy standing next to me rolled his eyes and snorted, "When I want chocolate, a Snickers bar will do just fine." She shot him an indignant look and stalked off.

What we all had in common was our love of chocolate—and that's where it ended. Once we got below the surface, everyone had his own ideas about what chocolate meant to him—and no one was budging from *his* standard, no matter what.

Several years later, I was in a company-wide meeting listening to our CEO lay out the annual new direction for the business. After the meeting, we all brought the plan back to our respective teams. As the plan worked its way through team meetings, town halls, company newsletters, and water-cooler talk, the original message got lost. We could all agree while flying at the thirty-thousand-foot level and looking down at the broad landscape, but we each had our own perceptions on the ground when we became preoccupied with the look of our own neighborhoods, so to speak. As multiple interpretations of the plan were set in motion, we were left with a lot of unintended outcomes—and disappointing results. The CEO was frustrated and other leaders were left scratching their heads.

Suddenly, I thought of the "Death by Chocolate" party. We had all gone to that party with a common objective—bring chocolate, eat chocolate, and be happy—only to be separated by our different interpretations or standards for what constituted "ideal" chocolate. What happened at that party was happening in our company—everyone had a different interpretation for what she thought the plan meant and how she would bring it to her team to implement. One woman's soufflé was another's Snickers bar. If a simple concept like chocolate could generate so many different opinions, attitudes, and points of view, how many more would occur when a complex strategy was at stake? When images and points of view differ and we can't communicate a consistent message, we wind up with a "meltdown." The outcome ends up looking like Snickers, truffles, and chocolate cake all mixed up together—the result isn't what we expected, and everyone is disappointed.

I see this problem all the time, and I'm sure you do, too. People get a thought in their minds after they hear something. They picture what it means to them. They talk with others based on their own understanding and they agree to take action based on that understanding, without considering how the originator of the message intended it to come across. To them, there was no original message—there is only the message according to their point of view, what they *thought* they heard. As a result, the original intention breaks down and, like the woman who walked away at the chocolate party, employees walk away confused and frustrated by these misunderstandings.

Have you ever wondered why two-thirds of all mergers fail to produce the value of the two stand-alone companies, let alone the additional benefits promised? Companies lose billions of dollars over Chocolate Conversations. Everyone talks at the "chocolate" level—what I call the *worldview* here—and they agree that they have something in common, the objective or result. Then the individual points of view kick in—what we'll call the *standards*—about what to do and how to do it, and these are different from team to team and from person to person. Everything melts down into a morass of upsets and complaints—these are the unmet needs I call *concerns*.

Only You Can Do YOU . . .

I knew I had something to offer when my former boss, Anne Mulcahy, who at the time was chief of staff and later became CEO of Xerox, told me that I had a unique talent. I was running a successful business, yes, but more importantly, I could "bring a diverse group of people together and get them on the same page." That wasn't the reason I was brought into Xerox, but when the company decided to make significant changes to its business model, Anne asked me to do just that and appointed me the "chief transformation officer." That was fifteen years ago. People had no idea what a chief transformation officer was, much less what I was meant to do. At the time, I'm not sure I knew. So when asked, I simply smiled and said, "I guess if you don't change, you're under arrest." That bit of levity gave me time to figure out what I *could* do to shape and facilitate the transformation from the "Copier Company" to the "Document Solutions Company" we wanted to become. That gig lasted five years and was the genesis for my company, *fassforward Consulting Group*, a business transformation boutique that I founded eleven years ago.

What matters to me is that people "get gotten." Every human being wants to be understood and validated. I've known this from my earliest years, when, as the middle child, I learned how to stand in the middle and not only survive but understand everyone around me—and get them to understand each other. I'm fascinated by people and their interactions. I love listening to conversations, even when they're happening at a table next to me in a restaurant. My husband often asks me if I want to join the other table. That's when we both laugh and I share the insights I've picked up from eavesdropping.

I hear not only what is said, but the silent conversation going on in people's heads—what they meant to say or wanted to say and couldn't. I often act as a proxy and say out loud what I think I've heard. It frees people to speak their minds in a way that respects another's point of view. I reframe conversations and situations so that everyone can understand everyone else, and I often move people to make a difference for themselves and each other. Growing up, I was told by someone very dear to me that I was a "translator." I didn't know I was developing a system for myself, but it's worked over and over again in every area of my life ever since.

That's why Chocolate Conversations resonate so much for me. I get it that people come from different walks of life—with different experiences, backgrounds, and origins—and where they come from defines them on a profound level. It's not simply what they believe, it is *who they think they are*. For leaders to make a difference all through the levels of their organizations, they must listen to, and understand, where people at each of those levels are coming from and communicate in language the teams understand so they can build real consensus. Leaders have to be more than good communicators, they need to be *translators*.

I've lived through several company-wide transformation efforts as a senior executive. In my consulting practice, I've helped many clients figure out how to take their businesses to the next level. You can't get there by doing more of what you did yesterday. You must constantly reinvent yourself, and that means change. Once I had the realization in that Xerox meeting that we were having a "Chocolate Conversation," I began to see Chocolate Conversations causing misunderstandings and serious meltdowns every time companies had to do something other than business as usual.

Let's face it: we *are* going to see ever-increasing waves of change in our digital, global economy. Change is really the only constant we face, and business as usual is a certain recipe for failure. *You're either growing or you're dying*—that's never been more true than it is today.

I guarantee that *right now* your competitors are thinking about the same three questions that global leaders of well-known brands, not-for-profit organizations, and, yes, even nations are asking:

How do we grow?
Can we scale?
Can we do it productively?

The question they often forget to ask, and the one the success of the other three depends on is: *Are we relevant?*

The answer is always, "Something's gotta change," and if something has to change, then someone has to lead people through that change. People have to understand what is being asked of them, and they have to see themselves in the picture.

That's why knowing what Chocolate Conversations are—how to recognize them and how to clarify them—is so important. You simply cannot change and grow your company while you're having them. Radical change absolutely guarantees countless Chocolate Conversations at every level of your company every day.

There *is* a way to have conversations that resonate for every person at every level, conversations in which each person sees himself as an important player in the new game. *And* there is a way to put change in context, get through it, and do it well. Here's how...

Three Rich Layers in This Book

The first layer in this book is about *change in companies*. We'll look at what works and what doesn't. We'll review why you can't just "use the wrapper"—some other company's playbook, business model, and organization design or its best practices—and wait to see the results. When I say it that way, people nod their heads, but it's surprising how many try to do this. And you can't stand still. Even if you are successful today, the path from industry leadership to receivership is brutally short. You have to find what matters inside and outside your company and translate that into the recipe for your relevance and growth five years down the road.

The second layer in this book is about **leading change**. Change starts with you. You're the one who has to make things happen. You have to be relevant to your team, your company, your company's strategy, and your customers. You have to figure out how you grow and scale within your company as you help your company grow and scale. *You* are the translator, moving from Chocolate Conversations to a deep understanding of where everyone is and how everyone fits so you can help get the company where it needs to be.

The third layer in this book is about **making change happen**. It gives you some practical things to do so you can change your company and achieve the relevance, growth, and scale you need to be a market leader. In a sense, making things happen as a leader is straightforward. Change happens in the conversation, and there are only two conversations that matter: conversations that *reframe someone's thinking* and conversations that *incite action*. Every other conversation is noise in the system, and the roar of that noise can be deafening.

The point of this book is to know when you are having Chocolate Conversations, to understand how to reframe the conversation, and to get people to act.

Change—even successful change—is bittersweet. You have to let go of a past that no longer serves your future. This is not losing who you are—it is taking what still makes sense, letting go of what doesn't, and having clear conversations that engage everyone in transforming "our" company. It's your job to clear the clutter and eliminate the noise in the system. The future of your company depends on it.

Death by Chocolate: Unwrapping Chocolate Conversations

A Chocolate Conversation has three main ingredients: *worldviews*, *standards*, and *concerns*. If you are unaware of these ingredients, you run the risk of misinterpretations and breakdowns in communication, a common pitfall in companies. In this chapter we will define what constitutes a worldview, a standard, and a concern and the importance each of these has in leading change and transforming a business.

A *worldview* is a series of images, assumptions, and beliefs that we hold about ourselves, others, and the world, based on our experiences. These perceptions shape the picture of reality we each carry around in our heads. We usually begin by adopting the worldviews of our parents, teachers, and early peers. As we grow and experience our world, we come to know our own capabilities and preferences, and these contribute to our evolving individual worldview.

I know from experience that when I talk, people listen—I can make things happen with words. I understand people and situations by listening and engaging in conversation. I know that facts and figures have their place, and understanding them is an important aspect of running a business. However, in *my* worldview, relying on numeric results as the only data points can cause a leader to miss important insights and shut down meaningful conversation.

Within that worldview of mine, I find that people who focus exclusively on the numbers trigger my skepticism. I have to work at not thinking of them as "bean counters"—I am aware that I do this, so I'm careful to keep from dismissing them out of hand.

There are people who are just the opposite. They find conversation too roundabout a way to determine what's going on. They'd rather go straight to the numbers to form their conclusions. In fact, if no numbers or hard data are involved, they are uncomfortable making an assessment and feel as if they're wasting their time. Over the years I've come to realize that hard facts can keep a conversation on track. Taking the emotion out of a conversation that has escalated can calm things down and clear up misconceptions.

My way of making sense of the world is no better or worse than any other person's. The way I am is a reflection of my own experiences and attributes, which I've become aware of over time. The challenge is that we also develop views about others based on our experiences, and this colors how we see them. My dismissing a person who is more comfortable with data and that person dismissing me because I'm interested in what's in people's heads are blind spots we both need to work on in order to understand each other. We each have vital information to relay to each other, and each of us has to find a way to hear what the other has to say.

Worldviews also extend to the larger environment around us. Some of us work in companies that have successfully focused on a core business or a product line, while others of us work for companies that have been successful through joint ventures. In the same way that our experiences inform the way we see people and listen to them, our experiences also impact how we evaluate new growth strategies. We will discuss different business models and their implications for transforming a business later in the book.

Standards are rules, codes, and guidelines that direct our actions in different situations. Like our worldview, our standards are developed through our interactions with others over our lifetime. Our standards serve as a direct route to our underlying beliefs and principles. As any developmental psychologist will tell you, basic expectations, like trust, are developed very early and are profoundly resilient. Others, like specific protocols for communication between adults in business, are learned over time.

Newer expectations will continue to be colored by older, more ingrained ones. Cultural examples are easy to see. Americans, for instance, place value on direct eye contact in negotiation to indicate honesty. However, you'll have trouble with this if you work with Korean executives, who come from a culture that considers direct eye contact to be rude. American and Korean standards are clearly different here. If you are not aware of this cultural difference, you may send strong negative signals before you've spoken a single word, and you'll have no idea you've done it.

You don't have to jump across continents and cultures to experience the awkwardness that comes from standards that are out of sync. I'm sure the majority of people we know in the United States would agree with the statement, "We should be hospitable when guests come to visit our homes." We run into different expectations when we add the statement: "We should always hug guests when they visit our homes." Some people would agree with this second statement as well. Others would qualify it by saying something like, "Sure, I'd hug my parents when they came to visit, but I think hugging my boss and her husband at the door would be weird." Some might consider physical contact, like hugging, to be an inappropriate way of greeting guests in general. Imagine how awkward it would be for someone who feels this way to get an unexpected hug.

Standards go far deeper than feeling a bit put off in a social situation. I've said many times: "When all things are expected, everything becomes a disappointment." Take a look at any problematic multibillion-dollar merger and you'll see this clearly. When AOL and Time Warner announced their merger in 2000, expectations ran high. The combination of deep Internet penetration with one of the largest entertainment content libraries in existence made this merger look like a dream come true.

Yet before the ink on the deal was dry, it seemed the new AOL Time Warner could do nothing right. There were massive culture clashes within the organization. The Internet people and the entertainment industry people had no common vocabulary. Because they didn't understand each other, there was no mutual respect. Within two years, the company had dropped "AOL" from its name, sold off the Warner Music Group, and fired CEO Steve Case, the architect of the merger.[1]

Time Warner had experienced the same trajectory once before. In 1991, when Time and Warner merged, expectations also ran high for that combined company. People expected big things from such a potent concentration of content and distribution channels, yet the company did not perform then either. The problems of 2000 had been foreshadowed in 1991: the Hollywood people didn't mix with the magazine people; the two sides dug in their heels and refused to work together. Nick Nicholas, the principal architect of that merger on the Time, Inc. side was pushed out within two years.[2]

Whether you're talking about Hewlett-Packard and Compaq or AT&T and NCR or one of the many other examples, combining a company based on the old, traditional economy with one sited in the new Internet world is tricky: everyone's standards kick in and the best-laid corporate plans can fail.

Concerns arise from information filtered through our worldviews and our standards. Our standards become our expectations. When expectations are not met, as in the case of the mergers we discussed, people express their disappointment. In some cases, these disappointments get expressed loudly and inappropriately; in other cases they're communicated passively. Either way, addressing concerns early on is critical to the success of any change. Ignoring them won't make them go away. Dismissing concerns can result in unintended outcomes like the failed mergers we are all too familiar with. Remember, a complaint is an expressed concern. Underneath every complaint is an unmet need.

Unmet needs will affect the way people act. Because actions put events in motion, uncovering concerns and addressing unmet needs are essential to the success of any change effort.

A worldview can be shared. Go back to the example we started with at the Death by Chocolate party: "We all love chocolate." At the party, each guest had her own standard for what chocolate she was going to serve and what chocolate she chose to eat. In other words, each of us brought our favorite sweet, thinking, "This is what chocolate *should* be." If we had all walked in to a table piled high with Snickers bars, the lady who wanted truffles would not have gotten what she wanted. She would have been upset because her expectations were not met. Many people can share a worldview, but standards are individual and personal. To avoid a Chocolate Conversation and its implications there are three *essentials:*

1. *Share your worldview:* what we will be, who we are, and where we are going. Share your vision, your strategy, and the new business model.

    a. *Vision is the dream.* It conceptualizes what the organization wants to be. It is a long-term view and concentrates on the future.

    b. *Strategy is the map.* It connects the dots from current reality to the future. State it clearly, laying out key milestones along the way.

    c. *Business model.* This defines the way the company or business unit makes money.

2. ***Establish and communicate your standards:*** this is the how, why, when. Explain how you came to your vision and how you expect others to participate in achieving it why it's important to the business, how, and when you expect it to happen. Standards are captured in the phrase: *"How we will make it happen."*

    a. *Operating model.* This is how we will run the business day to day—how we will execute the strategy and measure our success.

    b. *Culture.* Culture is the value system of the organization, the principles we live by, and the way we treat each other and our customers. It's *"The way we do things around here."*

    c. *Communication.* This is what we say, how we say it, who receives the messages, and when. It's expressed as message discipline and *"Message discipline drives operational discipline."* Keep communication simple and clear.

3. ***Uncover concerns:*** Actively seek feedback. It's better to know what's on people's minds than to let things fester.

    a. *Anticipate what could go wrong.* Encourage people to ask questions. *Ask* if there are any concerns. Where do *they* see potential pitfalls?

    b. *Make the undiscussable discussable.* Talk about your concerns, and say things that give people permission to express their concerns.

    c. *Don't shut people down.* Mean it when you say, "No question is a dumb question."

Change Happens in the Conversation

Rick Thoman said something a few years after being fired as CEO of Xerox that made me pause. He told an interviewer from *The New York Times* that he was bewildered by the criticism of his leadership at Xerox. He said that the difference between the successful turnaround at IBM and the failure at Xerox was that "...IBM people were ready for change. They weren't ready at Xerox."[3] I was stunned by this comment. Whose responsibility was it to get people ready for change?

People are never ready for change. They might hope for it, they might fear it, they might deny that it will ever come—but they are never ready for it.

Thoman wasn't ready to lead change in a company that wasn't IBM or to do what was necessary to get people ready for change. His job as the new leader was to have the two conversations required in any change agenda: the conversation that reframes *people's thinking* and one that *incites them to action*. That's what Lou Gerstner did at IBM and it's why his leadership there is legendary to this day.

Gerstner placed some strategic bets, for sure—and let's talk about what he did to make those bets pay off. Gerstner took his worldview and translated it through the company. He had direct conversations with everyone on the inside, and those conversations mirrored the ones he was having with people on the outside. He was very clear about having his expectations met. Sometimes the conversations were tough. IBM's transformation was fraught with resistance from the old guard. Gerstner stayed on message. He laid out, in simple, direct language, his standard for the way the new order would play out. The IBM business model is now twenty years old, yet product-based companies looking to become services companies are still using it as their blueprint for change.

The "best practice" business is one of the cornerstones of the multibillion-dollar U.S. consulting industry. It's easy to see why. Thriving companies, from Apple to IBM, continue to be targets of "best practice" analysis. Drawing on a winning story—like Gerstner's at IBM—can be helpful *if* you fully consider the nuances and culture of your own company. Simply adopting the IBM model and using it as a recipe for transforming your business is not a good plan.

Let me illustrate what I mean by that. I'll compare IBM with Xerox, which did just that: Xerox, the copier company, tried to copy the IBM model.

Can I Have Your Playbook, Please?

IBM is particularly close to my heart. I never worked for the company, but I worked for Xerox, which used IBM as a benchmark when it needed to turn the company around. Yet, despite copying the IBM playbook, installing IBM's number-two guy as the successor to our CEO, and taking people from their roster, our efforts were a high-profile failure.

Both IBM and Xerox were shaped in their early golden age by a big gamble on a new product that fueled explosive growth. In both cases, the company subsequently dealt with a humiliating fall and had to face a turnaround situation. However, the turnaround stories were very different, despite the fact that we, at Xerox, were consciously trying to do what had just worked for IBM. Let's take a look at why IBM succeeded and why copying the playbook didn't work for us.[4]

The golden age of IBM was fueled by the creation and production of the 360, a powerful computer introduced in 1956 by CEO Tom Wilson. The 360 yielded explosive growth and profit. In addition, IBM then bundled and sold its software as a separate product, creating what would become the multibillion-dollar software industry. IBM was the computer company to end all computer companies, offering signature hardware and software to a world clamoring for more.

It worked for a long time and only started to come apart

as IBM failed to envision what Steve Jobs and Steve Wozniak imagined very well—that regular consumers, rather than businesspeople, would become the next big segment of computer customers. IBM's failure to face the challenges from both personal computers and the new small network servers, combined with a growing intracompany conflict, resulted in a decline that seemed almost insurmountable.

By the late 1980s, IBM was in very deep trouble. It had more than four hundred thousand employees who were heavily invested in an increasingly outdated business. The company had introduced a PC that was not competing with Apple's or others' in the increasingly lucrative consumer market. IBM's internal organization was enormous, expensive, and slow. Company earnings had been steady at the $5 billion level in the late 70s and early 80s. By 1989, earnings sagged to a mere $3 million. IBM also had a growing consumer relevance problem. By the late 1980s, Apple, Gateway, Dell, and other competitors had an increasingly robust line of products that did exactly what consumers wanted at an attractive price point. Apple became the darling of graphic designers and creative people because of the ease with which you could get it to do things like draw without having to memorize the DOS command book. Others companies, like Dell, competed very aggressively on price. Wang was an early competitor whose menu system was far superior and easier to use than IBM's. Apple's graphic user interface (GUI) was so user-friendly that consumers wondered *why* IBM didn't have a better version. Microsoft was well on its way to becoming the software giant it is today, creating a multibillion-dollar business niche in developing IBM-compatible software with good GUI. While it may be hard to believe, the whole software business was once IBM's to give away.

John Akers was brought in to try and pull this once great company back together. Akers felt that IBM had to shut businesses that were no longer part of its core. IBM sold its typewriter, keyboard, and printer businesses, and renewed focus on the PC and server business at the expense of mainframes. It didn't work—everything Akers tried failed to halt the decline.

Chocolate Conversations about what belonged in IBM's core business ran rampant, while erosion in all product lines turned into a hemorrhage of money. In 1993, IBM announced an $8 billion loss for fiscal 1992, which was then the largest single-year loss in U.S. corporate history. Between 1991 and 1993 the company lost nearly $16 billion. The three-decade-long golden age started by Tom Wilson in the 1950s seemed to be over. Thousands of IBM employees lost their jobs, and Akers was one of them.

Lou Gerstner came on board in April of 1993, signing on as CEO of a company Bill Gates said would be closed and forgotten within seven years. This was the first time since 1914 that IBM had hired an outsider to take the top slot. Gerstner had been chairman and CEO of RJR Nabisco, a top executive at American Express, and a management consultant at McKinsey & Company, but he had never led a technology company.

Gerstner treated IBM like an accident victim on an operating table, and his first priority was to stabilize the patient. IBM had been on the verge of selling the mainframe business when Gerstner arrived, but as he performed triage, he quickly became convinced that mainframes were really the key to IBM's survival. IBM could provide end-to-end solutions for large businesses better than anybody else because of its own size and experience. This was beyond the capabilities of Apple, Compaq, and Dell. Fighting Apple and others on the PC front, on the other hand, seemed to Gerstner to be a losing proposition.

Gerstner bet the company on solutions instead of PCs. As had Watson in the 1950s, when he bet on the 360, Gerstner placed the right bet. Focusing on solutions put IBM back in the black by 1994 with a profit of $3 billion.

Lou Gerstner wasn't interested in just stabilizing his patient. He wanted IBM to become the great, innovative company it had once been, a true industry leader. Gerstner's strategy was to shed commodity businesses and focus on high-margin opportunities. The company regained its standing among institutional purchasers by building up its global services business, which rapidly rose to become one of the leading technology integrators.

Gerstner was brand agnostic—IBM would integrate whatever technologies the client required even if they came from an IBM competitor. This was unheard of in the former IBM culture.

Gerstner's IBM is a great turnaround story, and he does a good job of telling it in his book, *Who Says Elephants Can't Dance?* What really impresses me is the way Gerstner avoided having Chocolate Conversations both with IBM's customers on the outside and leaders on the inside. It's great to have a new strategic direction that really catches customers' attention, but it's another thing to get an organization of tens of thousands of people spread across the globe to actually deliver on it.

Gerstner handled this elegantly with a program he called "Operation Bear Hug," which was meant to restore faith in IBM among key customers. Gerstner required each of his fifty senior managers to visit at least five customers and get feedback about the machines they were using. If customers voiced a problem, the top leadership team met, together with anyone in the enterprise who could help fix the problem. The idea was for customers to know they were the most important consideration in the development of any IBM product. It was also a powerful way of drawing people who had vital product or process knowledge into the conversation and linking them to what customers wanted, needed, and liked.

Gerstner had a powerful way of engaging his company. He wanted the voice of IBM's people to be heard in the boardroom. He wanted all employees to see for themselves where the company was going, why it was going there, and what it would mean to each of them personally. Gerstner focused on making sure IBM employees could *see themselves in the picture*. He developed a dialogue through an internal messaging system to communicate with just about everybody in the company.

His outreach efforts were galvanizing. In a company culture that was hierarchical and filled with entitlements, he *didn't* simply say, "Follow me," he demonstrated, "I'll go first!" He took the artwork off the walls and eliminated the executive lunchroom—everyone ate in the same employee cafeteria. Employees were encouraged to have a direct dialogue with Gerstner. They could share their *concerns*, and he listened. More importantly, he did something about those concerns. The organization was more united in its direction by the late 1990s than it had been in twenty years. This is a potent lesson about the power of people seeing themselves in the picture— and becoming change leaders themselves as a result.

Gerstner had been CEO for about three months when he stated in a press conference, to the astonishment of all listeners: "The last thing IBM needs right now is a vision." Gerstner felt that IBM had all the vision statements it needed—what customers and IBM employees alike needed was *action*. Communicating directly with customers and with everyone inside the organization was top priority: he engaged everyone in a future they could live into. The results were dramatic. Today IBM does over $86 billion in sales and operates in more than 160 countries.

When Xerox ran into trouble a few years after the IBM turnaround, those of us working at Xerox naturally looked to Lou Gerstner's plan as the best example of how to recover. However, we tried to follow his strategy playbook without first thinking about cultural implications. A lot of companies make this mistake—it's easy to see when someone makes a strategic play in the market. It's harder to see what is going on in the organization's culture and internal conversations that allow it to *deliver* on the new strategy and make it sustainable.

As leaders at Xerox, we fell into this trap. After all, we were the "copier company"—our motto was "We can make any copy look just like the original." It was more than a slogan, it was our worldview. Our company culture was built around this worldview. We thought we could simply copy Gerstner's playbook and yield the same results.

We were impressed by what Gerstner had done to rebuild IBM's relevance, fuel growth, and take advantage of its scale. We didn't think about the implications of "Operation Bear Hug" or Gerstner's internal communications efforts, and we didn't acknowledge how much energy Gerstner invested in dealing with the culture of IBM.

IBM Got the Brass Ring and Xerox Didn't

I believe it's because Xerox *didn't* pay attention to the conversations inside and out, while Gerstner did. Let me tell you a little bit about Xerox and why I believe Chocolate Conversations were the reason we failed.

I joined Xerox because at the time it was a high-growth business that valued salespeople, and I knew sales. I came in on an accelerated management track and, through several moves, led a division and later moved into my created position of chief transformation officer. I was in a unique position to observe what was going on in the company. I was privy to what our CEO and his management team were doing (or were trying to do), I was in touch with the concerns of the employees, and I was attempting to bridge both worlds. I realized I was witnessing Chocolate Conversations everywhere, and in that moment I saw why IBM's turnaround worked and why our attempt wasn't working. What I saw and heard about what worked and what didn't forms the basis of my consulting practice and, now, this book.

The trouble started for Xerox in the 1970s, when Japanese competitors began using Chester Carlson's selenium drum technology. As long as Xerox had proprietary rights to the technology at the heart of Carlson's process, there was no way to produce dry copies as well as Xerox could. When the selenium drum came off patent, Japanese competitors scrambled to make high-quality, lower-priced dry copy machines. Xerox began losing both market share and money rapidly.

At the same time, Xerox had invested heavily in its Palo Alto Research Center (PARC). PARC scientists invented things like the graphic user interface (GUI) and a computer mouse that perfected earlier versions from the German company, Engelbart. PARC assembled one of the earliest PCs, the Alto, which would form the basis for the later Apple computers of the early 1980s. However, Xerox seemed unable to bring any of these inventions to market.

Steve Jobs visited us in the early eighties. When he saw all the things PARC had developed, his comment was that *Xerox scientists and marketers were treating these inventions like fancy toys instead of like the future of Xerox.*

Steve Jobs did what Steve Jobs does. A master of consumer relevance, he was imagining what customers could do with these "toys" and how they could be monetized. Apple considered buying Xerox in the 1980s, then opted for a much better deal—for Apple, at least. It bought the rights to the computer mouse and the GUI and launched the massively successful Macintosh line of computers. Jobs succeeded where Xerox failed simply because Apple knew how to make what Xerox invented relevant to customers.

In the meantime, Xerox was fighting for its life. Our CEO, David Kearns, realized that the Japanese were well on their way to putting us out of business. He knew that price and quality were important to customers. Kearns was astounded by how poorly Xerox was equipped to deal with competition. The company's explosive growth had been a trap. Xerox had gone for fifteen years without a meaningful competitor, and it had come to control 90 percent of the copier market by the early 1970s. By the end of the 1970s, that market share had collapsed to 14 percent.[5]

Kearns was an extroverted and outgoing guy, and quality became his mantra, an almost evangelical mission that sparked a global turnaround. He and several of his senior executives went to Japan to see what our competitors were doing. He came back fired up with ideas for how Xerox could outdo its Japanese competition. He traveled all over the company and met with members of the organization from top to bottom. He personally inflamed them with his zeal. It worked. The message was simple and clear and people understood it: "We *can* do it better and we can do it for the price customers want and we can be great again!" Kearns stayed on message and, when he was on a roll, people could *see* themselves in a different future.

Kearns led Xerox to win the Malcolm Baldrige National Quality Award, which recognizes U.S. organizations for performance excellence. The company was steadily regaining market share when Kearns reached Xerox's mandatory retirement age in 1990. He turned the helm over to his successor, Paul Allaire.

Allaire was a Xerox insider who had worked for the company since 1966. He was handpicked, but he was no Kearns. Introverted and introspective, he couldn't be the evangelist for change that Kearns had been. While he believed that quality was vital, and he knew that focusing on what was relevant to the customer was important, he was also sharply focused on Wall Street. He wanted to deliver shareholder numbers that had been Xerox legend ten years before.

While he didn't take his eye off the ball, he did throw another one in the air. Restructuring and redesigning companies to maximize potential was a big trend in the 1990s, and

Wall Street loved those restructurings. Allaire redesigned Xerox substantially, and it impressed analysts.

Allaire also saw the emphasis that IBM and others were placing on "solutions" businesses. In 1994, Allaire rebranded Xerox as "The Document Company." The idea was that sophisticated document handling linked to the growing power of desktop computers was the wave of the future. The emphasis on quality continued, the structure of the company was redesigned, and the strategic focus of the company changed.

However, the *people* in the Xerox organization were floating further and further out to sea. Kearns had been an evangelist, having conversation after conversation within the company and with its customers that sparked a global turnaround of Xerox when the company needed to focus on quality. In contrast, Allaire's focus seemed to shift to profit, no matter what. In the absence of leadership conversations, the corporate restructuring and new brand identity were confusing to the Xerox organization—and Chocolate Conversations emerged everywhere.

The confusion inside the organization was matched by increasing customer confusion. Customers didn't understand what "The Document Company" meant for them and they were not confident in the solutions proposed by Xerox. The complexity of some of the proposed solutions made it hard to deliver high-quality, reliable systems. Ironically, Allaire's sharp focus on profit and Wall Street metrics—at the expense of the internal conversation—led to a decline in revenue and stunted growth.

Allaire seemed to make the right step in 1997 when he hired Rick Thoman from IBM. Wall Street certainly liked the choice—the announcement of Thoman as Allaire's intended successor caused a nearly 3 percent bump in the value of the stock. Thoman had worked with Lou Gerstner at McKinsey and had been part of Gerstner's IBM turnaround team, heading the Personal Systems Group. The IBM turnaround was big news at the time, and Allaire clearly thought he was bringing some of Gerstner's secret recipe to Xerox. In 1999,

Thoman became CEO of Xerox, while Allaire retained the title of chairman of the board.

Thoman was a smart man. He held a doctorate in economics and three master's degrees, in addition to his credentials as part of Gerstner's IBM turnaround team. Yet, perhaps as a result of his cerebral understanding of the business, he was unable to communicate his ideas to Xerox's people in a way that allowed them to see themselves in its future.

When people say, as many have, "Thoman failed because he was an outsider in a tightly knit culture," I reply that David Kearns was also an outsider. The difference with David Kearns was that, under the wrapper, Kearns was a guy who made it his business to find out what was needed, go there, and take people with him.

You couldn't get under Rick Thoman's wrapper—if you didn't get his cerebral take on what a Xerox solutions company was, he became impatient and curt. Thoman hired a small cabal of like-minded people and, instead of getting the message out to the organization, he and his crew became inwardly focused, effectively cutting off any conversation with anyone else in the company—and with customers.

There was no Operation Bear Hug at Xerox. Neither Thoman's emphasis on knowledge within The Document Company nor the shift to vertical sales teams was *relevant* to customers, and Thoman and Allaire wouldn't admit it. By the time Allaire fired Thoman, after only thirteen months as CEO, Xerox had lost a staggering $20 billion in market value.

The prognosis for Xerox was not good. Thoman's successor, Xerox insider Anne Mulcahy, felt the sales reorganization was "poorly implemented," and she imitated David Kearns in personally connecting with the organization to stabilize it. However, Xerox remains committed, a decade later, to a solutions business that trails far behind IBM's. The stock price has never recovered and growth remains elusive. The patient is off life support, but Xerox is not the company it once was.

Best practices are not a proxy for understanding what is happening in your company. Lou Gerstner recognized what we refer to as Chocolate Conversations, and knew they were happening between IBM and customers and inside the company as well. The actions he took addressed these conversations. Xerox tried to follow Gerstner's footsteps without understanding the Chocolate Conversations Xerox was having *in its own organization*, and its change effort was a costly failure.

How can you avoid making the same mistake? There are a lot of things Lou Gerstner did that are worth emulating. Some of what Xerox was trying to do to expand its copier business into a broader digital document solutions business made sense. However, the success or failure of the change is in properly assessing the worldviews, standards, and concerns of your company—and getting everyone on the same page.

Lou Gerstner came into IBM and saw it for what it was—a "follow the leader" culture. He knew he'd have to do something to show his people and his customers that he understood what it would take to align with them, so they would be open to hearing and following his message. Hence, the artwork came down off the walls, the entitlements disappeared, and he made himself accessible.

At the same time, Gerstner's message was loud and clear. He created a vivid picture in the minds of employees and customers alike, and he carried them along with him. He stayed the course. He made things clear. He didn't allow confusion and he didn't stand for outliers. It's the most important part of what he did, and it's the most intangible. He lived through the bittersweetness of the change.

You don't find this in the strategy or the structure of the organization. There is only so much structure you can redesign. There is only so much process you can reengineer. Eventually, you have to change the way people think. You find this in the way people in the organization talk to each other.

In contrast, Xerox was a "consensus culture"—everything was

done by committee. Thoman never did acknowledge that people were not going to line up just because he said so. Trying to layer what Lou Gerstner did at IBM over a different culture—a different worldview—was a breeding ground for Chocolate Conversations that Thoman didn't know were happening. What's more, he didn't know these conversations needed to be addressed and reframed because he didn't think he should have to deal with anything other than what he said. That was his downfall.

So how do you make change happen in your organization? You have to change the conversation—and that's where the chocolate comes in. Successful transformation isn't just a matter of changing the ideas and the strategies.

Think about this: David Kearns intuitively placed a bet on quality and then brought his top people to see what he had seen. He inspired a picture in their heads that was the same one firing his imagination. Kearns's enthusiasm and personal commitment took hold, and his team joined him in taking the message throughout the company to outline clear objectives that would have a direct impact on customers and increase the market share of the company. The intangible things Kearns did were a lot closer to Lou Gerstner's playbook than what Allaire and Thoman did. Why? Because Kearns understood the power of conversations and knew how to bring people along with him in those conversations.

Thoman tried to make the same strategic bet Gerstner did, using the imaging base of Xerox as a platform for end-to-end document solutions just as Gerstner used the mainframe business at IBM as a solutions platform.

Thoman failed because he never acknowledged the distinct and contrasting worldviews of the two companies. The different standards of Xerox employees as well as those of the Xerox customers were overlooked. When the concerns surfaced, it was too late. Thoman was publicly ousted, the old guard lost credibility, and we failed to achieve the success everyone had hoped would follow the change initiative.

The conversations that happened everywhere in Gerstner's IBM—and in Kearns's Xerox—were absent from Thoman's regime. Thoman wanted to reinvent Xerox: he tried to find what really mattered in the Xerox business and the unique flavor the company could bring to market. And here's the thing—these were the right places to start. The strategy was there, but the implementation was not: Thoman failed to reframe people's thinking and therefore did not get people to act in a way that would make a difference for the business.

You can't change the structure and expect people to act the way you tell them to. Changing the compensation model won't get them there either. To get people "ready for change," they need to embrace *your* worldview, understand *your* standards, and *be allowed to openly express their* concerns.

Allaire and Thoman had a Chocolate Conversation from the beginning. When Allaire asked Thoman to come on board, he was prepared to mentor him and gradually transfer power. Thoman believed from the onset that he was "in charge" and he acted accordingly. Allair continued to engage in the business and weigh in on decisions. For those of us observing the transition, we could see the disconnect between these two leaders and the executive team they were both governing. Mixed messages were coming through the senior staff and the leaders from each line of business were confused. This confusion traveled through the company. It became obvious to those around that the two leaders were divided. They continued having Chocolate Conversations with the organization—and didn't know it.

Even though it all went wrong, Allaire and Thoman were asking the right questions: Do we need to reinvent Xerox? If we do, what needs to change and how do we do it? The next two chapters in our conversation will focus on these two questions. We'll see the role worldviews, standards, and concerns play in all the things we are trying to do.

Mergers & Acquisitions:
A Petri Dish for Chocolate
Conversations

Hanging on to a business model that is no longer relevant—and that can't scale beyond where it is today—is a recipe for slow growth and perpetual cost cutting. These environments are ripe for Chocolate Conversations among employees and customers—people know when a company is standing still. Employees want to work for successful companies and customers want to do business with successful companies.

Figuring out *what* needs to change means taking a hard look at your company culture and owning up to "how things get done around here." It's important to understand what you need to let go of—that model, culture, or "sameness" that no longer serves your future is the first step.

So, how do you do that and transform your company?

Many companies do this with mergers and acquisitions (M&As). It is a fast way to add what you need. The rationale goes like this: "We have products and a distribution system that company X wants, and company X has a technology and a delivery system that we need to grow. Let's get our companies together and we will dominate the market." This is a *1 + 1 = 3* deal—the whole is greater than the sum of its parts. The capabilities that each company has are critical to both companies' long-term growth *beyond* what either of the companies could have achieved on its own.

The reality is, for two out of every three mergers, the story usually ends with 1 + 1 = ≤ 1. The merged companies perform way below expectations. On a people level, synergies fail to develop, key people leave, customers complain about dislocations in delivery, and value is lost. On a company level, scale fails to materialize, productivity falters, and companies shrink instead of grow.

Sometimes, companies lose their identity in mergers and their relevance evaporates right along with it. Why? It falls

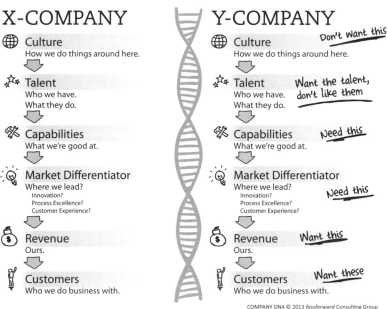

X-COMPANY

⊕ Culture
How we do things around here.

⚚ Talent
Who we have.
What they do.

✂ Capabilities
What we're good at.

💡 Market Differentiator
Where we lead?
Innovation?
Process Excellence?
Customer Experience?

💰 Revenue
Ours.

👤 Customers
Who we do business with.

Y-COMPANY

⊕ Culture   *Don't want this*
How we do things around here.

⚚ Talent   *Want the talent,*
Who we have.   *don't like them*
What they do.

✂ Capabilities   *Need this*
What we're good at.

💡 Market Differentiator
Where we lead?
Innovation?   *Need this*
Process Excellence?
Customer Experience?

💰 Revenue   *Want this*
Ours.

👤 Customers   *Want these*
Who we do business with.

COMPANY DNA © 2013 *fassforward* Consulting Group

Figure 2–1: Company DNA

right back to the Chocolate Conversation. The companies came together because they bought into a common worldview. Once the deal is closed and the euphoria of the newly formed entity is behind them, they find that the culture and the standards are different, and they don't know how to get value out of the new company. Figure 2-1 outlines why two companies came together and where the two companies often disconnect after the merger.

Both companies want the capabilities of the other to enhance their own. They wanting to retain what is best about both of them, *and* they want to add new capacities to create that synergistic "greater whole." Both companies want to retain their own customers *and* both companies want to add new ones so that the new company grows beyond what either could have done alone. These two pieces are where everyone agrees.

But—and this is a big "but"—their cultures are different, and culture begets language and "how we do things around here," so basically the two companies don't understand each other from the get-go. *And*, that "different culture" hired talent that blended with its own culture and standards, so each company finds that it doesn't like or appreciate the talent that the other company brings to the table. Yet it is this very talent that has created the value for each of the companies in the first place.

In the two examples we'll highlight in this chapter, I'll talk about what happens when different cultures with conflicting standards come up against each other and we'll look at how to navigate through that phase. I'll show you how to discover *what* you need to change and *how* you can drive that change across your entire company, even if your company spans the globe.

Successful Mergers Merge Standards

Estée Lauder Companies was *fassforward*'s first client. I met and worked with Harvey Gideon when he was the head of R&D at Revlon, and reconnected with him when he took over R&D at Estée Lauder. He brought me in and laid out the company's dilemma.

The strategy for the company was to acquire popular brands that attracted a broader, younger consumer so it could fill the void left open by its own customers growing up. One of those brands was a hot, new, Canadian line, MAC cosmetics. MAC, or Makeup Artist Cosmetics, had been founded in Toronto in 1984 to supply professional makeup artists. As a pleasant and profitable surprise, the company found a consumer base—and opened its first store in New York in 1991.

Estée Lauder Companies acquired MAC only seven years after that. It seemed the perfect product line to appeal to a younger demographic—MAC was famous for its dramatic color line and popularity among hip urbanites. It was miles away from the traditional upscale department store brands, the greatest of which was Estée Lauder.

My first meeting was with Gideon, Lauder's head of R&D, and his chief scientist, Shahan Nazar. Nazar talked to me about the challenges he faced mixing MAC's young, "first to market" culture with Lauder's long-standing, world-renowned, scientifically based way of doing things. Nazar wanted to bring the best of both companies together. MAC would bring speed and innovation to Lauder, and Lauder would bring scale and a global presence to MAC.

One thing immediately caught my attention. I was having these conversations with Gideon and Nazar in 2001 and the MAC acquisition had been completed in 1998. We were talking about the things the companies *would* do for each other, which made it clear to me that the integration of the two companies hadn't happened yet.

When I met with the Canadian team at MAC and subsequently with the Long Island team at Lauder, it was clear they both bought into their marriage at the *worldview* level. Both companies were committed to broadening reach in the younger demographic and both were confident they had the products to do it.

However, their *standards* for how they would work together were not in sync. MAC described itself as a "bad girl" company—fast moving, not tied down, edgy, breaking the rules. Lauder, on the other hand, prided itself on being the "good girl" company—dependable, sophisticated, delivering consistently year after year, and playing by the rules. The team at MAC felt unappreciated and, in some cases, trivialized for not being a long-standing brand with a world-class research team. The team at Lauder felt that MAC saw them as outdated and rule-bound. The Lauder team chafed at the idea that MAC did not respect their years of experience and groundbreaking scientific innovations.

I could see that these two groups were having a classic Chocolate Conversation.

The more I talked with both teams, the more I could see the common worldview. It was understood that MAC would bring relevance and new growth. Lauder would scale the brand globally and introduce cost-effective research practices that would improve productivity. Both teams shared and agreed with this worldview. This was the basis for the two companies coming together.

Things broke down when each company realized it had different standards for how it would bring products to market. The companies also had different work practices and compliance standards. Having the same worldview and yet being unable to deal with different standards led to frustration on both sides. This happens frequently when merged companies are as clear on the worldview as MAC and Estée Lauder were—both sides wind up questioning the other's commitment to the shared foundation because the different standards come across as roadblocks and people lose patience with one another.

So what do you do when you reach this point? You do the same thing inside the organization that you would do *outside* if you were having a Chocolate Conversation with your customers. You find out what's going on with people by talking to them and hearing their concerns. Remember, behind every concern is an unmet need. When you lead a company in this kind of situation, your first priority is to uncover those unmet needs and figure out how to address them. Those unmet needs will tell you what part of the picture is missing or is distorted in people's minds. You'll get all the clues you need to stop this Chocolate Conversation from going any further—*if* you talk to people and find out what is really going on with them.

We met with the head of MAC Research and key members of his team to better understand their operation, current practices, and business model. Next, we met with Nazar and others on the R&D side of Estée Lauder. From our interviews, we produced a themed synthesis we refer to as *rapid insight*. A themed synthesis comes from taking the raw feedback received in the interviews and categorizing common responses under a topic for discussion such as innovation methods. The themes are category headings and the feedback is synthesized under those headings. Providing the synthesis to the leaders and their teams gives them *rapid insight* into what's on the hearts and minds of the team and its members. These interviews were conducted by *fassforward's* anthropologist, Doctor Susan Anderson. They uncovered the standards and concerns of both groups and provided the foundation for the work we needed to do with the teams.

A two-day workshop conducted with both teams let us work through the issues both companies were having with leveraging each other's expertise. First, we put together a "go forward plan," outlining a few well-focused actions to execute the plan. After breaking the team up into cross-company pairs, we had them read through the synthesis point by point. Then we asked them to highlight what was hurting their progress and what could advance their progress if each side made some concessions. The most important part of this workshop was that both teams came together to understand their standards and figure out what they were going to do about them—without sacrificing the value of MAC's "bad girl" image *or* Estée Lauder's "good girl" image.

That was eleven years ago, and this is what Nazar had to say in a recent conversation:

> Recently, our CEO hired former Proctor & Gamble VP Carl Haney to be Harvey's successor. He is working alongside of Harvey and with me to eventually take over the operation. I brought him to MAC in Canada for a visit, and he was very impressed with their operation and integration into Estée Lauder. He saw how smoothly things were running, how well people from MAC R&D and Lauder were working together and bringing innovative products to market. He asked me what the secret to the success of this acquisition was over some of the others he's experienced. I told him the three big insights we uncovered and acted on as a result of our work with *fassforward Consulting Group:*
>
> 1. The two brands are like two people who come together to form a relationship and become a couple. Each has their individual identities and personalities and then there is the identity and personality of the couple. They needed to establish that third identity and personality without diminishing each other.
> 2. If they were willing to acknowledge and adopt the best of what both companies brought to the table, "all boats would lift."
> 3. Lastly, we recognized that we needed a well-respected integration manager who would be a liaison between the two brands. It took me a while to convince Harvey that this was a needed and a viable full-time position that would more than pay for itself. It did.

The first point—establishing a "third identity...without diminishing each other"—is exactly where merger integrations go wrong. I see one company swallow another all the time. I also see companies limp along with different teams pulling in different directions because legacy cultures are still alive years after the merger. Creating a third identity is what gets you to 1 + 1 = 3. The third identity is what makes more out of the partnership; a merger is more than just the two companies now appearing on the same P&L. Newly merged companies need to do three things in order to make this happen:

1. Get the people who shared a common worldview when the companies merged to talk about their cultural differences and address their standards head on. You can't let different standards simmer and turn into serious concerns.
2. Have teams work together to identify and work through focused actions that will embrace each other's standards and help create the third identity.
3. Appoint an integration manager and give that person the resources she needs to do the job.

As a note here, I have seen some companies employ a full-time integration manager and a small, effective integration team with members drawn from key stakeholders across the company. These groups worked together productively for two years, which is a great investment in the future of the combined company. When you think of the cost of a failed merger, every dollar spent on these teams is a sound investment.

Always remember where the information to make things work comes from: talk to your people. Listen to their concerns. Behind their concerns are the answers that will help you clear up confusion and get things back on track.

An Unlikely Merger Inside an Acquisition

Several years ago, while working with the executive team at Interpublic Group of Companies, IPG, *fassforward* collaborated on a multi-agency project referred to as *New Realities.* The findings from the project were gathered into a white paper that was made available to the holding company's agencies and their clients. The research centered on the new realities facing marketing and media companies in the digital age.

During this time, IPG was looking to bring the best of its portfolio to current and potential clients. One consideration was the merger of Draft Direct and Foote Cone Belding, FCB. Draft Direct Worldwide was a successful direct marketing company founded in 1978. Draft was acquired by the Interpublic Group of Companies in 2000 along with several other well-known agencies. FCB, also an acquisition of the holding company, is the world's third oldest advertising agency, dating back to 1873.

One of our executive sponsors was the CMO for IPG. Bruce Nelson introduced me to Draft Direct Worldwide, and Laurence Boschetto, then President of the company, currently the CEO of Draftfcb.

When we met with Boschetto, he and the Chairman of Draft Direct were discussing the benefits of a merger with FCB. They came to the realization that the two companies would be *better together.* The opportunity to completely redefine the way agencies engaged clients was very appealing and Boschetto was keenly aware that clients were asking more from their agencies. Clients wanted a business partner that could help them solve their business problems. They wanted to understand consumer behavior, how and why consumers identified with their brand, and the influence of social media on their consumers. Clients also wanted to measure the return they were getting on their investment with their agencies. The newly formed Draftfcb later addressed this client expectation as the *Return on Ideas*. Boschetto saw how Draft, a direct marketer that was consumer-focused, and FCB, an ad agency that understood and promoted brands, could bring together the right capabilities to achieve what they referred to as "a new breed of agency." The new merged "Draftfcb" would address the new realities of a digital age.

Traditional Advertising agencies were referred to as "above the line" and direct marketers were referred to as "below the line." In advertising, "above the line" companies use media that are broadcast and published to mass audiences, while "below the line" companies use media that are more narrowly focused, tailoring messages to a niche audience. Draft Worldwide was a successful "below the line" agency, and FCB was a well-regarded "above the line" agency. Creating this *"new breed agency"* would completely redefine theses lines, eliminating the distinction for both the agency and the clients. *fassforward* described this as the merger that *dared to cross the line.*

The change involved addressing two big cultural norms: the "below/above the line" distinction, and the walls between agency and client disciplines. *The merger that created Draftfcb was predicated on the idea that an agency could work through the lines and offer marketing solutions that solved business problems. These solutions could be fully integrated or discipline specific depending on the needs of the client. In a collaborative and productive way the agency could bring its full capabilities working with each other on behalf of their clients.*

Breaking down the divisions between Draft and FCB and between the disciplines in each company was critical to the success of the new model. Breaking down the walls between the disciplines in the marketing functions of their clients was another big hurdle. Everyone had to buy-in to make this work—all while the two companies were merging. This was a Chocolate Conversation waiting to happen!

Boschetto brought *fassforward* in to facilitate and collaborate with selected taskforce teams to flesh out the new business model and map out the strategy for making it happen. One of the outcomes of the work we did on behalf of Boschetto and the teams became affectionately known as the *Blue Board*. This was a visual illustration of the consumer and market realities and how the new agency model would address them. Boschetto was so adept at taking people through the *Blue Board* that it became widely received and posted in every office around the world.

Another key output from the taskforce was the formation of the *Wheel*. The wheel was a symbol of eliminating lines and fostering "round table" collaboration. It brought all the disciplines in the new Draftfcb together. The wheel was designed to "...bring together the art and the science of marketing."

We worked with a cross section of leaders to identify challenges in implementing this new way of working. Socializing the new Draftfcb model had to take place for 10,000 employees in ninety-six offices spread across six continents. We worked with Boschetto, his senior team, and the taskforce leaders to develop and deliver a custom workshop that would fully explain and demonstrate the new business model, the wheel team design, and new ways of working to every merged Draftfcb agency across the globe.

We built the chocolate exercise into the wheel workshop. In this exercise, we started by asking participants to conjure up the picture in their minds that appeared when they heard the word "chocolate." Next, we asked people to write on a Post-It note the first image that came into their minds. After everyone wrote something down, we asked for volunteers to read their responses. People would always smile as they heard what others said. Through hundreds of these sessions over the years, I've heard responses that range from M&Ms to gourmet Belgian chocolate to a Chocolate Labrador retriever.

As they shared results, people laughed at some of the associations made in the group. The next question we asked was the clincher: if a simple concept like "chocolate" can evoke so many interpretations, how did the group think something like the "wheel" would be interpreted by the ten thousand people who had to work together to make it happen? This was a great icebreaker for these meetings, and it helped surface the standards and concerns quickly. Boschetto was then able to address these concerns on the spot.

People around the globe would call out a *chocolate conversation* when they heard one. It became code in the company for, "we are not on the same page." We would hear people at all levels say "we're having a *Chocolate Conversation*."

The wheel workshops were followed up by webinars, supporting materials on the company intranet site, and quarterly visits to support—and case studies to show—proof points. All this was implemented to translate the message in as many different ways as was needed to unbundle chocolate conversations and reinforce standards and address concerns.

The essence of the model and how to work with it was consistently communicated and practiced on in all ninety-six offices around the world. *And*, the application was tailored to be relevant to the local market. Boschetto used the metaphor of the Chocolate Conversation in his presentations all over the world. It was amazing how different the standards for chocolate were in cities like New York, Chicago, Rio, Dubai, Johannesburg, Mumbai, and Shanghai.

Boschetto understood cultural nuance and was not rigid about applying the U.S. standard for implementing the new model. In his words:

> "You don't want to dumb it down, but you don't need an exact translation either. You are looking for the essence—a platform and philosophy for how we work that is balanced with what is appropriate to each region globally."

Boschetto got the metaphor of the Chocolate Conversation when he first heard it, and why the concept of the chocolate conversation resonated across the globe. Everywhere we went—in multiple languages—people were breaking down worldviews, standards, and concerns. We established global standards with local flavor.

Speaking with Boschetto recently about this book and discussing our experiences together, he said to me:

> "When you understand the subtleties of Chocolate, you get the dilemma that any company involved in a transformation faces. The nuance of language brings different views, and these views can undermine everything we are trying to do. Understanding standards and concerns and dealing with them right, at the outset are vital to successful change."

Within a year of the merger Draftfcb won Kmart, the new client saying that Draftfcb was uniquely qualified to meet their needs. We had the opportunity to facilitate a working session with the Draftfcb client team and the Kmart marketing team, led by Boschetto and their CMO. We used the chocolate conversation as an icebreaker and were able to establish a common worldview for the relationship, standards for how the teams would work together, and an approach for how the teams would address concerns as they arose.

In October 2008, *Ad Age* focused on the state of the agency two years after the merger, saying:

> "In the two years since the Chicago-rooted agencies Draft and FCB merged, the agency has won more than 250 pieces of business around the globe, including Kmart, Beiersdorf, Discover, SeaWorld and the U.S. Census Bureau."

People in other agencies began clamoring for Draftfcb's playbook.[1]

Though that's a great compliment to get from peers, Boschetto understood what we've talked about in this book. It's

less about the playbook and more about the unique challenges you face, the way you talk with your people—inside
and outside—to find the path that works for that unique set of
issues. I come back to what Boschetto said earlier: *"When you
understand the nuances of Chocolate, you get the dilemma that any
company needs to change."*

I have shared two examples from two very different companies that made change happen. Both companies had strong,
committed leaders who understood that change is never easy,
that it happens in the conversation, and you have to be the one
to lead people through it.

Addicted to Relevance

Growth, scale, and productivity have always been at the front of leaders' minds. Traditionally, corporate leaders look for new ways to grow and take advantage of their scale. As we discussed in the previous chapter, if companies aren't growing fast enough on their own, leaders will look to a merger or an acquisition to expedite growth. Many of these companies will take significant productivity measures to maintain profitability. This means cutbacks and reductions in force, commonly known as RIFs.

The big question—the one that *should* be keeping CEOs up at night, but which is seldom asked—is *"Are we relevant?"* Do customers want what we have? In reality, customers and shareholders will answer that question even if you're not asking it.

In the case of Xerox and IBM, both CEOs recognized that the products they were offering, once new and innovative, were now commodities or were things customers no longer wanted or needed. You don't get growth without relevance. When companies are growing, they can take advantage of their scale and leverage productivity to achieve profitable growth.

When I think about the context of any company's transformation, I think about what makes a start-up take off. There really isn't a difference between a new company and a company that is transforming. You need to start by offering people what they want and what they are willing to pay for—those two aspects will tell you what's *relevant* to them.

For example, in the 1950s and '60s, cars were it! Everyone who could drive wanted one and did whatever it took to get one. The automobile industry served a massively expanding market. Another example is Motown; in the 1970s, the music industry posted gain after gain because vinyl records—remember those?—were the thing everyone wanted. With the advance of technology, we can see a progression from one "Have to have it!" to the next. In the 1980s it was computers, in the 1990s it was mp3 players, and in the 2000s, smartphones and tablets. In contrast, the mega-empires of the 1950s, like GM and Sears Roebuck—which didn't remain relevant—are on life support.

The mere passage of time doesn't rob you of relevance. It's what you do when it's your time to do it. For example when digital photograpy hit the market, Kodak, a well-respected company with a long history in photography had its own "*Kodak moment.*" They didn't get on board, missed the digital market, and lost their relevance and their market leadership. They didn't do what they could have done when it was their time to do it. Alan Mulally has revitalized Ford Motor Company, saying, "Everybody says you can't make money off small cars. Well, you'd better damn well figure out how to make money because that's where the world is going."[1]

The key to launching a business and then reinventing it time and again is an obsession with *relevance.* And that means change. Relevance is the catalyst for *growth*. This is a universal truth that stretches from political careers to products to services to ideas.

Relevance is an idea or a product whose time has come. When someone hits on a political idea that is relevant to people, it spreads like wildfire and a person can become a national figure overnight. Look at how quickly the Occupy Wall Street movement grew into a nationwide phenomenon from a single demonstration in a cramped New York City park. Remember how fast the Berlin Wall fell and Soviet authority vanished in Eastern Europe. The powerful U.S.S.R. dissolved when the *idea* that things could really be different took hold. We all watched on the news as the Arab Spring ignited massive change in Tunisia, Egypt, and Libya.

Now move that concept to business. Look at how quickly people embrace technologies they never knew they needed mere months before. Some of these innovations, like Google or Facebook or YouTube, are ideas that connect people and content. Others, like the iPhone, are devices that provide an environment in which social networks happen. All of these ideas have created new markets, disrupted old ones, and generated billions of dollars of growth. These sectors did not exist a decade ago. Businesses that are not relevant may hobble along, but they will eventually fail and may end up in receivership.

As I write, Ford is making a strong comeback while the Facebook IPO has lost 30 percent of its value because investors are questioning exactly how it can be monetized. *Relevance doesn't just mean "new" or "digital"—it is what connects people to something they care about.*

The Great American Chocolate Conversation

Eight years ago a young, passionate senator from Illinois started a conversation with the American people at the Democratic National Convention. We were intrigued. He captured our attention with his ideals and his candor. Whether we agreed with him or not, we listened and we heard something that stirred many of us. That resonance set the stage.

Two years later, he had another conversation with us, a conversation about change. He told us up front that it wasn't going to be easy—we would face hardships and challenge.

He made it clear that if we wanted to reclaim our relevance in the world, grow our economy through innovation and education, increase jobs and productivity, and scale our influence by building relations with our foreign neighbors, things had to change. We bought into the conversation—his worldview was our worldview—and though he was not the candidate of choice for some, we elected him to the highest office in our government. Barack Obama became president of the United States and the leader of the free world.

Why?

He was relevant to a broad audience. He used contemporary and conventional methods to reach us. Young people engaged in a conversation, most for the first time, with a soon-to-be global leader, through social media—blogs and Facebook. You could invite him to join your network on LinkedIn and he accepted. He bridged the generation gap. He was approachable to young people and credible to an older generation.

What he said mattered. He stayed on message and scaled that message across the globe. He brought people from all walks of life, from all genders, ethnicities, and ages, to the conversation—and it wasn't a Chocolate Conversation.

Obama came with a worldview that resonated on a deep level for so many people—jobs, change, integrity, growth, respect, and leadership. He spoke of a country we could be proud of, one that, family by family, gave increased value for all. His message was relevant. He was relevant.

What happened to that conversation? Do the people of our nation and of the world believe that they are still in the same conversation with him? Do they believe they are in *any* conversation with him? People wanted that worldview played out according to their own standards and that's often not how things seemed to go. He stopped engaging with us, and the result is Chocolate Conversations everywhere. When people are left on their own to think about what is going on, it is natural for Chocolate Conversations to emerge.

What I'm saying has nothing to do with endorsing a presidential candidate, his policies, or his platform. I'm talking about how a message that started out as clear and engaging to a broad audience eventually deteriorated into Chocolate Conversations all over the nation.

Successful businesses experience the same sort of deterioration. You can find yourself in a Chocolate Conversation with your customers and your employees that is every bit as derailing as one in the political arena we just discussed. When you disappoint your customers and fail to meet their standards, they go elsewhere—*fast*.

Forty years ago, a well-known retailer named Sears, Roebuck and Co. told its customers through its advertisements that *the customer is king*. Customers believed that message because the salespeople in the stores delivered on that promise. The conversations Sears was having with its customers mirrored the conversations its employees were having. The worldview *"the customer is king"* translated throughout the company. Customers' standards were met so well that Sears became a household name and a revered brand. The company was relevant, growing, and had national scale. The biggest retail presence in the country, I remember hearing that Sears was responsible for 2 percent of total US GDP.

What happened?

Walmart came on the scene and Sears scoffed at it. After all, it was *Sears*. As Walmart offered better prices and an acceptable customer experience, Sears changed the conversation. The new focus was on profit and price point, and the customer was no longer king.

Earlier this year, I heard Sears mentioned on the radio and realized I hadn't thought about the company in ages. It was contemplating selling off its Lands' End subsidiary to get enough cash to keep going after years of decline in store traffic. The company has gone ten years without turning a profit. It's not relevant any more.

Customers still buy what Sears sells. They just don't buy it from Sears anymore.

What "Addicted to Relevance" Means

I was having a conversation with a client about Steve Jobs a few years before Jobs passed away. The usual stuff came up, such as Jobs's relentless focus on user experience, simplicity, and elegant design. My client asked me what I thought was the key ingredient to Jobs's success. I quickly replied, "He's addicted to relevance." That really got my client's attention—and when I heard the words come out of my own mouth, I did a double take as well! It's what got me thinking about the significance of *relevance and why certain companies succeed and others don't.*

Relevance was what Steve Jobs was all about.

When Jobs returned to Apple after the NeXT venture in 1996, he believed that the key to customer adoption was simplicity, ease of use, and beautiful design. He called Apple's developers together and asked what they were working on. He put a hold on all their projects and directed them to work on four straightforward challenges: build the best possible consumer desktop and the best portable computer for consumers and do the same for business. That's two products for two market segments. His strategy was so basic that everyone in the company could immediately get it, work on it, and succeed.

Keep It Simple

Apple's late 1990s and early 2000s computers for both personal and business use dominated the market, and for good reason. The message of *simple and elegant*, which was embedded in Jobs's conversation about Apple's strategy, was carried into the company's design solutions. It was the keystone of the marketing campaign. The conversation inside the company became the conversation with customers. From strategy to design to marketing to sales to service and customer experience—*simple and elegant* played all the way through. It is a vital part of the reason Apple is the most relevant consumer brand today.

Simplicity is part of the consistent *feel* of Apple products. Hipness, an ergonomic sense, user-friendliness, state-of-the-art design, edginess, high quality, and sensitivity to customers' wants are standards that permeate everything that bears the Apple logo. The experience of everything Apple makes or does is consistent across the board. You sense it in the iPhone now, just as you could in the Macintosh nearly thirty years ago. Think of Apple computers, phones, music devices, and now data storage and backup capabilities through iCloud. Customers trust that Apple will meet their standards and exceed their expectations in anything the company does. Relevance has always been what makes Apple, Apple...*It's the thing about a constantly changing company that has never changed.*

The Four Considerations of Business

I remember Steve Jobs coming into Xerox in the early 1980s to look at our Alto PC, which we had never launched in a commercially viable form. Jobs had an uncanny ability to see what people would want and need before *they* realized they had any need for a new technology. What made it work was that Jobs had a team of people who had the same worldview, standards, and concerns that he had.

As the Apple team talked, you could almost *see* the lights going on above their heads. There was no Chocolate here— they all had the same idea at the same time, and the picture of how to make it real was consistent among them.

Our Xerox team, on the other hand, was nothing but Chocolate Conversations regarding the new technologies. It's why we could never market our own technologies successfully ourselves—we couldn't figure out a clear message about what this technology was for or why you would want to part with a thousand dollars to get it. Jobs could hear our Chocolate Conversations and recognize them for what they were. That's part of why his interest in buying Xerox quickly faded and he bought only the technology he needed instead.

Earlier, when I talked about Xerox's desire to imitate Lou Gerstner, I made the point that you can't turn your company around by borrowing someone else's playbook. Jobs had the same halo around him Gerstner had twenty years ago, so the urge to imitate him and turn your company into the next Apple is certainly there. But imitating Apple won't help you anymore than lifting Gerstner's playbook helped us. We need to think about how relevance fits into the bigger picture—and we need to translate how it fits into *your* picture.

We've sifted through the ingredients that make up a Chocolate Conversation—the worldviews, standards, and concerns

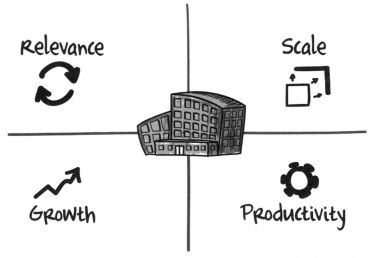

4 CONSIDERATIONS OF BUSINESS © 2013 *fassforward* Consulting Group

Figure 3–1: Four Considerations of Business

that are crucial to the way people see what needs to be done in any organization—and we've explored why those elements are important to every conversation. Now, we'll take a further look at what all businesses need to do to grow. We'll prove the declaration I made at the beginning of this book—that everything to do with leadership and change happens in the conversation. And, it happens in the context of what I refer to as the four considerations of business.

As I've said, many leaders haven't put "relevance" at the top of their list. When Paul Allaire brought consultants in to help turn Xerox's business around, the conversation and initiatives were all about productivity. I remember talking to Anne Mulcahy and saying the back channel feedback from employees is that "Productivity is a code word for cutbacks." The initiatives were being touted as a way to make the business more efficient. People weren't buying it.

In the 2008 recession, I saw lots of companies introduce similar productivity measures. I've also seen companies spend millions to restructure the business in order to gain scale. Mergers and acquisitions are frequently driven by the desire to extend reach into new capabilities, geographies, and markets. Some companies, like International Paper, have "growth by acquisition" strategies—they just keep digesting more to fuel their own expansion in the marketplace.

Growth, scale, and productivity are all valid goals of business; however, the strategies companies employ to achieve these goals often breed Chocolate Conversations throughout the organization. And Chocolate Conversations can cost a company its relevance—people inside and outside the company lose track of the story. If what you do is not relevant to your employees, it won't be relevant to the customers they serve. If relevance *isn't* one of your business considerations, you'll find growth and scale difficult to achieve, and productivity will be about shrinking your company.

Struggling with Relevance

I've spoken to groups of leaders over the past few years about Steve Jobs's addiction to relevance, and sometimes I get the reaction, "Well, if I launched a product like the iPhone, I'd have it made," or "Yes, but he just filled a really good niche." I don't think either of these observations is on target.

Let me talk about "filling a niche" first. Ten years ago, the U.S. Congress passed the No Child Left Behind Act. People had been worried about the quality of the American education system for years, and No Child Left Behind was meant to give state education departments clear guidelines for standards-based education. Teachers were to be accountable for student performance according to clear standards in areas like math and language arts, so that all American school children would advance.

One effect of the new law was an explosion in the number of companies offering standardized test packages to state education departments. Companies like Pearson, Kaplan, and the Educational Testing Service (the folks who bring you the SAT) rushed to enter into lucrative state government contracts to provide testing and scoring services for millions of schoolchildren. Today, dozens of providers, large and small, make up this testing industry, which is really just a niche created by a single federal law.

However, a revolution is about to happen in U.S. standardized testing. In 2014, for the first time, several states will implement tests built around common core standards. The fifty separate states *had* been running their own testing programs, but 2014 will mark the start of several states sharing one test package based on the common core. The majority of state education departments are talking about the huge savings they can reap as soon as they transition to one nationwide standard.

Two vendors, newcomers to the testing industry, have

already sewn up the common core contract, a development that is expected to shut most existing vendors out of the industry within a few years. So how did the newcomers get the contract? They come from the online survey industry. They successfully made the case to the state boards of education that online tests provide an interactive environment far better suited to evaluate student capability than the old paper and pencil "fill in the bubble" tests.

Things like this happen all the time in business. Someone sees a niche and fills it. And the market changes over time. The person who displaces you might not have been in the same industry last year, or may not even have been in business for very long.

For state education departments, the demand ten years ago was "Hey, get me standardized testing I can use to comply with No Child Left Behind." Now, because of the rich lives students are living in online environments and the appearance in classrooms of hardware like iPads and tablet computers, education directors are rethinking learning and testing environments. Someone savvy enough to read the changing conversation and take part in it can secure an enormous amount of business.

Steve Jobs bet on user-friendly personal computers aimed at consumers wherever they might be. He didn't have the bias toward businesspeople in office settings that everyone else did at the time. Computers for personal use were part of Apple's explosive growth, and you might think of it as a niche. Jobs gave consumers a PC that enabled them to start writing, banking, gaming, publishing, drawing and designing—and this was before the Internet linked all these activities to a wider world.

Jobs didn't tie Apple to one product line the way many technology companies do or the way No Child Left Behind testing companies have—and this is an important point. You can dominate your market for years, only to find yourself pushed out because you've gotten comfortable in your position. Jobs moved from computers to iPods, and made Apple a player in the music world.

There was a time when Apple *never* would have gotten into music. Back in the 1970s, the Beatles objected to the name of the new Apple Computer Corporation because the Fab Four's record label and umbrella organization was called Apple. Jobs signed an agreement with the Beatles' Apple, allowing him to use the name because he was running a computer company that would never have any overlapping music or media interests, so there would be no confusion over the two companies' products.[2]

Then...Jobs looked at the Sony Walkman and had another epiphany about something consumers could use that wasn't on the radar yet. The early Sony Walkman played cassettes and later morphed into a CD player. However, the Sony Walkman was limited because it could play only an album's worth of material, maybe a dozen songs at best.

Jobs asked his designers, *What if we could give people a thousand songs with digital quality in a device the size of a credit card?* Why not carry your entire personal music library around with you everywhere you go? This was the idea behind the iPod. Since introducing the iPod in October 2004, Apple has dominated the digital music player sales market in the United States, capturing 90 percent of the market for mp3 players and over 70 percent of the market for all types of portable players. In the first quarter of 2008, iPod sales accounted for 42 percent of Apple's revenue, followed by 21 percent from laptop computer sales and 16 percent from PC sales. These are significant numbers.

The added good news is that after a number of escalations in the lawsuits from the Beatles' Apple Corp, including, over the years, settlements, appeals, agreements, and payments to Apple Corps paid by Apple Computer—finally, there was a happy meeting of the minds—and in 2010, the companies announced that seventeen official Beatles albums were made available for sale on Apple's iTunes Store.

Think of how long IBM was married to the mainframe business. Mainframes were the company's cash cow for twenty years, and they were the platform for building the solutions business that served as the bedrock of IBM's next period of growth. IBM actually withheld new technologies from the market, sometimes for a few years, to let service contracts on existing products run their course. Xerox also based its prosperity on the basic 914 copier idea for twenty years.

Apple is different—the company is completely willing to replace innovative products that still have life in them if there are new ideas and products that can change customers' lives. In other words, *Apple is willing to cannibalize its own niche markets to launch something new and exciting, effectively staying ahead of the curve on relevance.*

Not satisfied with a strong home PC market, Apple launched iBooks, then iPods, then iPhones, then iPads, then iCloud—all in pursuit of customers' collective tomorrows.[3] Look at the future as Apple sees it: the company expects iCloud to become the backbone of its revenue in the coming decade, moving the business from devices to online storage capacity and online environments.

So what's going on in this company? Is it that Apple had the luck to hit on killer products several times in a row? I don't think that's the story at all. Jobs's relentless addiction to relevance, *and* his insistence that the company itself stay relevant, is the core worldview of Apple.

This is a company that seems to have very few Chocolate Conversations. There is a real line of sight from worldviews to standards. Apple people get the message, and that message carries through to customers. Apple users are simply not interested in hearing what other computer companies have to say. Apple speaks directly to them—to the worldview and standards *they* have as end users.

According to Millward Brown Optimor's ranking of the Top 100 Most Valuable Global Brands, as of May 2012, Apple is the number one most valuable brand in the world, at $183 billion, superseding number two, IBM, at $115 billion.[4] It's hard to call such a huge business a niche company, but if Apple has a niche at all, it isn't in products, it's in *relevance itself.*

What's critical about being addicted to relevance is you don't even need to make a product. Think about YouTube. This site started as a file-sharing protocol that a few people put together so they could exchange videos online. Only a few years later, it had become so universal that Google bought it from its developers for a billion and a half dollars. YouTube has completely changed the face of music and video. It's grown to be one of the primary ways in which new music and video artists become known.

Marketing for traditional feature films is also changing rapidly because of YouTube. The blockbuster Ridley Scott film, *Prometheus*, put up advertising for the android featured in the film, marketing a product the film imagines will be available in about eighty years! *Prometheus's* viral marketing generated enormous buzz, even though the plot of the film was a closely guarded secret.

LinkedIn and Facebook are additional examples of platforms people never knew they needed. The spread of social media from college campuses to, well, pretty much *everywhere* in the past decade is changing the way people interact, get jobs, sell *anything*, represent themselves, and meet potential spouses.

Yet, we keep getting pulled back to earth by practical concerns. Part of Facebook's ethos has always been *quality of the experience over commerce.* The site was developed with the quality of the user experience paramount and commercial concerns put off to the side. The reward has been nearly a billion Facebook users. Think about that: one human being in six is involved in this thing. The downside is that stakeholders can't figure out how to monetize it.

General Motors pulled a $10 million advertising account from Facebook right before the IPO, and the offering itself has been rocky. I am writing this book a few months after the offering, and Facebook stock has dropped from the opening price of $38 a share into the mid $20 range. The big question is, can you keep the flavor of Facebook and still sell advertising space? Is conventional advertising relevant to Facebook users? It remains to be seen, but no one can doubt the company's relevance as a social site, even as it scrambles to make its IPO worth the money.

You can be relevant and remain a more traditional business that does well in both bricks and mortar and digital worlds. Barnes & Noble is a great example of this. Many bookstore chains, notably Borders, have folded in the past few years because they weren't able to compete with online stores like Amazon and hadn't embraced the growing e-book phenomenon. People don't want to take the time to visit a store when it's so easy to go online and have the purchase arrive the very next day, or even the very next minute with a digital download. Barnes & Noble has invested heavily in its own Nook e-reader and revamped its retail stores with Nook showrooms, free Wi-Fi, and amenities like Internet cafes and Starbucks coffee kiosks, making the store experience richer than simply browsing racks of books.

At the same time, B&N's website is well put together. It is cross-referenced well, and fulfillment is exemplary—clearly the company has put a lot of effort into making sure the feel of the website reflects the flavor of the stores. By moving into the online environment without fear and maintaining the same flavor online that is found in the stores, Barnes & Noble has ensured its ongoing relevance while many of its competitors have failed.

As for loss of relevance, the American record industry is a perfect example of a once-huge business that never saw change coming. Record labels had almost a "can't go wrong" bet in the 1960s and 1970s. Companies like Warner Communications were making billions in the glamorous rock-and-roll and disco worlds.

And then Napster appeared. Its revolutionary file-sharing technology virtually destroyed traditional record labels. Although the original peer-to-peer Napster was shut down by court injunction for copyright infringement, the concept of file sharing in the form of mp3s that was at the core of the original Napster technology started a revolution in how music could be sold and played. The original Napster declared bankruptcy and its brand and technology was sold off in bankruptcy court, but the technology survived—and is thriving.

Now, all the young people I know buy their music online via that same mp3 technology from iTunes, and even upstarts like Google Play and Spotify. Napster, itself, was sold off to Roxio and is now partially owned by Best Buy through a deal merging Napster with Rhapsody and is in the marketplace now as a fee-based online music store with its brand intact: Napster, a Rhapsody company.

While file-sharing and copyright concerns remain complex issues, the point is that traditional record labels lost relevance with consumers because they failed to envision the future iterations of the music business. The record industry has become locked in a series of high-profile lawsuits with its own recording artists over adequate payment for digital rights.

Digital music has made it possible for the iPhone and the iPod to generate billions of dollars in revenue for Apple and create hundreds of millions of delighted consumers. The music industry doesn't seem to be able to figure out how to plug into this consistently growing market. Instead, the industry is locked in acrimonious arguments with its own artists and customers, many of whom cannot see why they even need record labels anymore. Not surprisingly, the industry has been shrinking sharply every year since the late 1990s.

The Curse of Success

Long-term success is a paradox. Success is what every company is looking for, but it is also a point at which many companies are tempted to stop having conversations with their customers.

Take Kodak, for example. In 1976, Kodak had a 90 percent share of the U.S. photo film market. It had been a titan for decades. So, where is Kodak today?

Kodak sharply underestimated the competition its products would face from computer printers, cell phones, and the Internet. None of these seemed to be in the same market segment, yet these were the very elements that linked together to serve and expand Americas love of photos.

In the 70s and early 80s, it was unlikely that anyone other than a futurist would have dreamed there would be a threat to cameras and film, based on early PCs and dot matrix printers. However, by the 90s, high-quality printers and digital formats were beginning to eat into Kodak's photo paper sales, and the first digital cameras were appearing. As a sign of the times—and one that Kodak should have taken note of—Dell began to give away digital cameras with its desktop computer/monitor/printer packages. These cameras were cumbersome, could hold only fifty or so pictures in their memory, and ate through batteries in just a few hours of use. But consumers loved them, and if Kodak had been engaged in active conversation with its customers, it would have seen an opportunity.

There was a strong desire for the immediacy and control of digital pictures coupled with the speed and versatility that Kodak products offered. Unfortunately, Kodak focused only on its core business, unwilling to incubate a digital arm that would eventually supplant the huge cash cow of its film and paper business. Kodak focused instead on preloaded film/camera packages, a new version of an old concept dating all the way back to George Eastman's day.

Kodak was a latecomer to digital photography and has paid the price. It hasn't turned a profit since 2007, went bankrupt at the end of 2011, and, in early 2012, announced it was abandoning consumer digital cameras to focus on corporate imaging. The company had already abandoned selling traditional film cameras.[5]

Looking back to 1976, it's hard to understand why Kodak failed to become the biggest digital photography powerhouse of the present. Follow the story forward, however, and you see that *consumer standards changed*. Kodak was not following the conversation closely and it missed the whole shift.

The worldview for both consumers and Kodak stayed the same: affordable, quality photos for the average, nonexpert consumer. The standards switched, though, with consumers desiring digital's speed and ability to control the image, and Kodak missed more than the boat. It missed a vital shift, and the ocean liner long ago sailed without them. The company became irrelevant, another analog casualty of a digital age. The Chocolate Conversation Kodak had with its customers cost it the whole company.

Staying in the Conversation with Your Customers

So how do you stay in the conversation with consumers and keep your relevance? For one thing, don't get comfortable no matter *how* successful you are. Businesses today can't stand still—competitors won't. The only constant we face in business today is change itself.

Look at what Richard Branson has done with Virgin to stay relevant and keep growing. Virgin began as a record store in the early 1970s—just *one* record store. By the end of the '70s, it was a major record label. Not a maverick move, really— recorded music grew at a strong pace from the mid '60s to the mid '80s and was glamorous. And, unlike the movies, records were inexpensive enough to make that you could actually get into the industry if you had a couple of bands that caught on.

Branson's real genius was in consumer conversations. Every time he saw customers in *any* business walk away disappointed, Branson imagined how he would have handled that situation. In the 1980s, when he saw customer demand for reasonable ticket prices in the deregulating airline industry, Branson and his record company launched an airline, Virgin Atlantic, hardly the move that other entertainment companies would have considered.

In the same decade, he sold his smaller record retail outlets and launched Virgin Megastores to capitalize on the consumer desire for a rich shopping experience, which he felt was poorly served. In 1992, he sold the Virgin Records business to EMI—he actually sold the most glamorous, oldest, seemingly most lucrative part of the company. He told the press that he had tears in his eyes as he signed away what many thought was the heart of his business.

This turned out to be a tremendously farsighted move. EMI paid the highest price for a record company acquisition ever negotiated up to that time. Only a couple of years later, the advent of file-sharing caused an implosion in the record industry, while Branson's Virgin Group became a venture capital conglomerate of more than four hundred companies with global interests in consumer products, transportation, and entertainment.[6]

The one constant, which has made Branson a billionaire and Virgin a household name, is the company's profound capacity for reinvention while retaining a hip and customer-friendly character. Branson knows how to have conversations with customers—and he's so good at it that it doesn't matter *what* business he's in.

The level of change at Virgin over the years might verge on the ridiculous—a bit like Hewlett-Packard abandoning the computer printer business or Kodak giving up on cameras. But think about where Virgin is today, compared with a company like Kodak.

Here's the bottom line: you can radically transform your company, like Richard Branson has numerous times, or you can let the market do it for you, as Kodak did. No matter what you do or don't do, and no matter how big and seemingly secure you are today, change *will* happen. You have to be able to guide that change yourself. If you are passive about what is happening to you, you'll become irrelevant, you'll be humiliated by how fast you shrink, and you'll become just another footnote instead of one of the main players.

How to Find Your Relevance

We've talked about why relevance is so important as a business consideration. So how do you do it? Market leaders have to ask:

- Are we relevant?
- Do our customers want what we have?
- Are we listening to them?
- Do we know what problems our customers have, and can we provide a solution?
- Do we need to change our business model?
- Are we easy to do business with—and if we're not, why not and how can we fix it?
- Do our employees know: Who we are? What we do? Why customers choose us?

When you can answer these questions and address the issues that will surface, you can begin a path forward that leads to renewed relevance and growth. I'll conclude this part of our conversation by emphasizing how closely knit relevance and growth are. Many successful small companies find out what's missing from the offerings of big companies and then find a way to be relevant in these niches. Their relevance both creates a market and fuels their growth. Like Steve Jobs, they create new markets in spaces that are underserved or completely overlooked.

Put it this way: scale and productivity issues are high-class problems when you are relevant and growing. Without relevance and growth, you have an anchor dragging your company down. Put your attention where it needs to be—get addicted to relevance.

It Starts with You

A few years ago, I got a call from a senior executive who was having trouble motivating his team. We met in his stylish chrome and glass office. I looked around and saw that the shelves in his office were filled with leadership books. Clearly, he was looking for the "secret sauce" that would make him a great leader. He had a brilliant mind—that was apparent from our first telephone conversation. He claimed his team couldn't keep up with him. He was frustrated, and I guessed that his team was frustrated as well.

He took me through the challenges his group faced. In speaking with me, he was very smart and expressive about what he wanted to achieve—I asked questions to help him further articulate his vision, but something wasn't sitting right with me.

Listening for the points in executives' business vision is what I do for a living, so I was able to read between the lines and get the whole picture. However, the very fact that I had to "read between the lines" at all meant that he wasn't speaking as simply as he could to communicate his vision and what he wanted his people to do. His conversation was peppered with what I call *corporate speak:* he wanted his people to be "information facilitators" and "system advisors" rather than sales representatives. I noted that he spoke over the ends of my sentences as if he couldn't wait for me to finish before he continued what *he* wanted to say, always a sign to me that someone is not really listening.

We met several times before he agreed to let me see him in action. I attended a staff meeting and watched and listened as he spoke to his team. I could see that he was trying to apply some of what we'd talked about. He was making a huge effort to incorporate my direction about speaking simply; however, the more he talked, the more he regressed into his normal corporate babble. He waved away the few brave hands that went up at the beginning of his speech, and soon everyone gave up and there were no more raised hands.

He spoke for one hour, during which he touched on a number of "key priorities." His message was convoluted and unclear. I watched his people as he spoke—many rubbed their eyes and foreheads, some looked at one another, wide-eyed, and I detected the slight shrugs between people that signal defeat.

At the very end, he asked for feedback. The silence was deafening. The group had long since given up trying to understand what he wanted of them. Some of them in the back actually put their heads in their hands.

When he concluded the meeting, his people didn't even seem to know that they could get up and leave—they stood up, looked at each other, and then slowly made their way toward the door. They left, not knowing or understanding what was expected of them—that was clear from the bowed heads, slumped shoulders, and quiet air of resignation as they filed out of the room.

When he and I reconvened in his office, I shared my observations. He bristled a bit and I could see that he prided himself on being an articulate, intelligent executive. No argument there—he was certainly intelligent. Among his peers, he probably was articulate. What he wasn't, was a good communicator.

Good communicators translate complex ideas into simple, straightforward language that moves people.

Leadership Happens in the Conversation

As a leader, you have a practical job to do. Leaders drive results through people. People need to pull together to meet targets and perform on behalf of the company and their customers. Shareholders and stakeholders want to be kept informed on trends and projections. It's all about people: the ones who work for you, the ones you work for, and the ones who buy from you.

For many years, I've been telling my teams, my colleagues, and my clients that leadership happens in the conversation. It's where you have the greatest impact as a leader every day. And, like chocolate itself, conversations can be rich, dense, and layered. What we say and what people hear can be very different. What we hear and think we understand can be misinterpreted.

Remember the great American Chocolate Conversation we discussed in chapter 3? President Obama opened a dialogue with a broad group of Americans and brought them along on the beginning of his leadership journey. He had a huge vision and, as soon as he became the president, he began to implement it. Shortly into his presidency, however, the health-care debate spun out of control and Obama seemed unable to control the spin and keep his message on track. Soon, even his own supporters became disappointed, as the conversation grew more shrill and adversarial. It may be true that some political issues—Social Security and health care and peace in the Middle East—are just explosive topics and no leader can guide a constructive conversation around them. I might agree because I have found that there are issues just as explosive in companies. As my colleague Gavin McMahon says, "Politicians are public executives."

I have seen significant controversy in companies attempting

to adopt a new technology that cannibalizes the core business, a shift that always causes different points of view to emerge. Changes in compensation benefit plans, and other reward systems are also fodder for controversy because they affect people on a personal level. Organizational changes can result in people losing power and influence—these may be positive changes for the company but may leave some people with ego wounds to lick. I don't have to tell you how brutal those conversations can be.

Leaders have to have those conversations—one on one, in small groups, or in a public forum. Conversations can take place in someone's office, over lunch, informally in the hallway, or formally in front of large audiences. Some conversations are televised, like webinars that CEOs have with far-flung global teams or even State of the State and State of the Union addresses.

There's no room for Chocolate Conversations here—all participants have to come out of the conversation knowing exactly what's changing, why, and how it will affect them.

The most brilliant change initiatives can die long, painful, expensive deaths. Chocolate Conversations erode people's confidence, performance, and faith in the company leadership. Ultimately, everyone suffers, and the company struggles to regain its footing in the same way our country and many nations around the world are struggling to regain theirs.

Having conversations that truly communicate what you intend is vital to achieving your goals and to surfacing the potential concerns of others. Conversation is so much the lifeblood of an organization that it can be said, "Communication is to leadership what water is to life."

At the worldview level, almost everyone agrees that communication is critical. When you go beyond paying lip service to this concept and you begin to set standards for how you communicate—with whom and with what frequency—you can do more to lead effectively and move your company forward than you can with any other initiative.

Leadership happens in the conversation, and that conversation happens in the moment. It is a choice we make. When you manage a project or a process, you have time to plan. When you are confronted with the unknown, you have to act in the moment and respond. Those moments often define our leadership. Even when we are silent, we are communicating. People will read into your silence as well as your words.

I will go further and say that communication is so central to leadership that once an individual becomes a leader, he no longer has the luxury of casual conversations. People hear everything. When you're a leader, the casual conversation that you have in the hall or the off-the-cuff remark you make could have significant ramifications. All of your remarks become part of the conversation your people are having; they'll have these conversations with one another, and they'll parse what you said, what you really meant, and why you said it. The senior leaders I consult with understand that every comment they make communicates volumes.

Communication needs to be authentic. It's not about saying the right thing or using the right buzzwords. One might say all the right things, in the right tone of voice, and in the most positive manner—and, it doesn't mean that those words will land as meaningful and true. Most people see right through someone who is talking in corporate speak or jargon. Speak straight, speak what you intend, speak from what you know to be true—and people will respond with their own conviction. You can then have a dialogue that is purposeful and moves your company forward.

If you think of every communication as a conversation and you are authentic and open, people will respond to you. Even when they don't agree, they will feel they can express themselves, and then you'll know why they disagree. This is a good thing. If you know that people disagree and you know why, you've opened a dialogue so that you can resolve the differences, align your people to you, and move forward into action.

You may not be the best presenter in the world, but if you are able to communicate in an open and conversational style, you will create receptivity and people will respond. You know people are responding to you when they give you feedback. This is how you uncover those unmet needs I talked about earlier. When you uncover the unmet needs of people, obstacles fall away and you are left with clear understanding that moves people to action.

Even the best communicators can be misinterpreted. It's important to communicate with the understanding that someone is on the receiving end of what you are saying. People are going to interpret what you have to say. Knowing that will encourage you to stay focused and speak straight from the heart.

I've met my share of superstar leaders, and even superstar leaders don't start out fully formed. Putting experience aside for the moment, the fundamental attributes that great leaders have is *the ability to convey a message to their followers that compels them to take action.*

Let's look at this for a moment. Napoleon, a short man with a grand vision, was able to conquer half of Europe. Winston Churchill, who successfully led England to resist Hitler during World War II, was a political outcast who spoke like he had a handful of marbles in his mouth. Golda Meir, a student who grew up in Wisconsin, established a nation state and led Israel solidly into the twentieth century. Nelson Mandela and Dr. Martin Luther King Jr. both challenged discrimination in their societies despite being the targets of prejudice themselves. Rosa Parks sat on a bus and, *in silence,* led a change that significantly advanced the Civil Rights Movement. Mother Teresa, through compassion and tireless effort, communicated with her devotion and faith to make a difference for the victims of poverty in India.

All these leaders had courage, commitment, and vision. But what really set them apart—what made them *leaders*—was their ability to convey a message to their many followers to take action. They spoke from their hearts about what they believed. People responded and made those causes their own. What made these leaders effective was their ability to convey what was important to them and make it important to others.

Speaking naturally and authentically about what you believe in, whether it is a political position, a personal choice, or a business decision, will get the attention of your audience.

People Who Make Themselves Heard

Thirty years ago, I visited GE's headquarters in Schenectady, New York. It was known then as General Electric, the company both I and my parents grew up with. It was a stodgy, old-line manufacturing company that made lightbulbs and small household appliances. When I visited the company's headquarters, I requested a ladies room. They were a little embarrassed because there wasn't one. I was escorted instead to a private executive restroom. It was already the 1980s and these guys were so far behind the times that they hadn't thought to provide an executive restroom for women.

Not long after that, a guy named Jack Welch came in and brought the company back to life. The conversation on the inside mirrored the conversation he and his leaders were having on the outside with customers, constituents, and shareholders. GE reestablished its relevance, grew year over year at astounding percentages, and scaled across the globe. Welch developed a well-deserved reputation as a master communicator, driving performance relentlessly through his ability to give people an unambiguous picture of what had to happen and where they fit in. During Welch's twenty-year tenure as CEO, GE's stock value rose 4,000 percent. Today Welch is asked to speak on talk shows and newscasts and to other corporations. His speaking engagement fee is $150,000. It doesn't matter that he's retired—he's still relevant, and he's still helping businesses grow.

To this day, GE is known for turning out superior leaders. Welch felt that if he focused on executive leadership, first by *walking the talk* and then by developing strong leaders, his executives could lead any business. He saw leadership as an expertise in and of itself, so much so that he created a leadership center at Crotonville, in Ossining, New York, which became the place to visit for any executive seeking to lead a business transformation.

The ability to reach your people is at the heart of your effectiveness as a leader. Over the past eight years, my consulting company has had the privilege of working with Verizon, its leaders, and teams across its businesses. Our first introduction to the company was through the Wireless division. At the time, the CEO was Denny Strigl. We never met with Strigl while he was at Verizon, but we did meet with his senior team and a cross section of leaders in operational and functional roles.

In these meetings, I was keenly aware of Strigl's influence. He immortalized a philosophy that he referred to as the "Shadow of a Leader," and leaders at every level of the organization *lived* it. His people often quoted him, and his pithy declarative statements, affectionately known as "Denny-isms," were firmly in the fabric of the culture. One of the many Denny-isms we heard was "The first job of a leader is to act." Another was, "Employees don't fail; their leaders do."

Strigl kept his messages simple and direct, and there was no ambiguity about his direction. He led and people followed. Strigl didn't have Chocolate Conversations. His worldview was widely known, as were his standards and concerns. One of his leaders told me that if you couldn't explain your direction on a half of a sheet of paper, you didn't understand what you were doing and neither would your people.

Lowell McAdam, now the CEO of Verizon Inc., was Strigl's chief operating officer. Although McAdam's style was different, he was a good complement to Strigl. Strigl's style was direct and declarative. He laid out a clear direction and people followed. McAdam's style is more Socratic. He asks thought-provoking questions that encourage people to problem solve and reach their own conclusions. What Strigl and McAdam have in common is that each of their styles is an authentic expression of who they are—and each of those styles moved people to action.

McAdam talked to me about his leadership principles. At the top of the list was integrity: "Always do what you know is right." This is not always easy, but leaders who live this principle are trusted and credible. McAdam is down to earth and real. He believes you can learn from anyone, and that includes people at any level of the organization. A highly approachable CEO, he spends time with employees across the businesses and the globe. He listens and he acts.

McAdam's advice to leaders looking to the next promotion is simple: "Do your current job." Leadership is less about ambition and more about bringing value to the business, your customers, and your team. Lowell McAdam lives these principles, and people follow and lead in his shadow.

One of McAdam's followers is Tami Erwin. I met Erwin in 2004 when we launched a company-wide leadership program within Verizon Wireless. She was a new regional president at the time and has since been promoted three times. We've worked with Erwin in each of her roles. Currently she is the chief marketing officer for Verizon Wireless.

Erwin's previous position was area president for the West. When Erwin took over the area, she faced several challenges. We met with the marketing V.P., and the rest of Erwin's team, her staff, and her regional presidents to work on an operational strategy. The intent was to translate the strategic goals of the company into actionable tactics that the frontline, customer-facing employees could run with.

The company's strategic goals made perfect sense to people at senior levels. Those goals needed to be translated for frontline employees so they could understand how to execute on them. This is where true leaders take it up a notch. Communication at its highest level is listening and *translating* the message across all levels of the organization. A good leader speaks to the "listening" of the various departments, levels, and concerns in the company. It's not enough to simply take the company line and assume that everyone's standards and concerns are the same as senior management's.

I'll show you what I mean. The table below illustrates what can happen if leaders simply parrot the same messages to employees at all levels in the organization.

What Happens When Leaders Speak the Same Way to Everyone

Strategic Imperative	What It Meant to Senior Leaders	What It Meant to Sales Reps *Fodder for a Chocolate Conversation?*
Widen the revenue lead.	We're leading our competitors, but we don't have enough of a jump on them; we need to make the lead bigger.	Get customers to buy more.
Reduce churn.	We're losing too many customers.	Our churn numbers are too high.
Lead in profitability.	We need to improve our margins and our PE ratio (price to earnings).	Uh-oh. It means we stop giving discounts to customers.

Many leaders believe their job is to simply pass on the message from the top, and they call that communicating, but I beg to differ. We've taken a very strong stand on this and said, "No, it's not. It's every leader's job to *translate*. You have a responsibility to translate the messages you're getting from the top through to your employees so that their interpretation is both consistent with the direction of the company and meaningful to them."

Working with the team, we coached them through the task of translating the corporate goals into clear terms that frontline reps could both understand and act on. They worked hard at it and what they came up with was amazing. Their response was, "Wow. This really hits home." You take each goal and you bring it all the way through the organization so that it matters to every employee. The table below shows how much more meaningful the translated messages were to frontline reps.

What Happens When Managers Translate Messages

Strategic Imperative	Translated for Sales Reps
Widen the revenue lead.	**Earn more dollars:** • Earn those dollars from your customers; they don't owe it to you, *and when you do:* • More revenue dollars for the company • More commission dollars for you
Reduce churn.	It's all about your customers—**Get 'em and keep 'em:** • It's great to bring new customers in, but you have to keep them and the ones you already have
Lead in profitability.	**Do the right thing:** • The right thing for the business • The right thing for the customer

So we ended up with a very simple, distilled message and actionable goals that became pervasive throughout the area. No one forgot them. They didn't have to be printed on a laminated card. People didn't have to sit and think about what they were told to do.

Gavin and I started with a premise that we ask all our clients to consider: *Message discipline drives operational discipline. Message discipline* is the term we coined to convey the importance of words. I think you have to be very disciplined about what you say, how you say it, who you say it to, and when you say it. The simpler you keep the language, the less likely you are to confuse people. If you keep your message simple and focused, and you target it to your audience, you are less likely to contradict yourself with confusing expressions that won't mean what you want them to mean to your people.

When we ask why people don't use simple language, we get confusing responses back. When that happens, I am even more convinced that it's because they know the message they want to convey but find it hard to do. Too often, the message gets lost because it takes a great deal of effort to make it simple. You know the old quip, attributed to Mark Twain, *"If I had more time, I'd write a shorter letter."* Distilling a message to its essence is an objective every leader should strive for. It reduces the risk of Chocolate Conversations. People end up thinking and doing what you intended.

The focus on message discipline grew out of a familiar complaint we were hearing from virtually all our clients: "We've got a great strategy. I wish I could get my people to execute on it." This was often followed by the comment, "They just don't get it."

My answer to that is, "If the masses 'don't get it,' who owns that? The leader owns that." If execution and operational discipline are critical to you, you need to understand that they're driven by message discipline. When employees get multiple messages—from headquarters, from regional directors, from their boss, each with a slightly different spin, they don't know what to pay attention to. *Message discipline drives operational discipline.*

Recently, in an interview with Erwin in her new role as CMO, we asked her to reflect on her journey as a leader at Verizon, and this is what she said:

> It is easy to assume a common understanding. It is the old saying: You assume and it makes an ass of you and me. In the haste to deliver, people assume understanding and a common background and they skip the step. They move to strategic planning and problem resolution without testing understanding. They do not clarify.
>
> I like the concept of Chocolate Conversations; it is simple; everyone understands it. It is easy to say how I think about chocolate and to see how someone else might think of a different chocolate.
>
> In our business, people come from different backgrounds and experiences; they have different skills and knowledge and understanding; they bring a different operational knowledge and strategic understanding. If you can get to a common framework, you maximize the differences. If you bring diversity and skip getting to a common understanding, if you skip the chocolate step, then you do not effectively communicate and you do not pull the different perspectives together; if you do that (skip getting to a common understanding), you do not deliver.
>
> People will ask if you understand; but no one will step up and say "I do not." Who would do that? And probably everyone thinks they do understand. Instead, we need to say, "Tell me your understanding." Then we can clarify by validation, not assumption. Tell me your understanding of the situation. If you ask: Does everyone understand? Everyone will think they do. You have to create an environment to say what you understand; then you get to the differences—then you can bring in each perspective; you can clarify and move forward.
>
> I do not care how great the strategy is or how wonderful the product is, if people are not valued, you can pack your

bags and go home. You treat your employees with respect, kindness, and integrity and the rest is simple. Think about our credo [at Verizon Wireless]; it is a culture of respect and constructive dissent. You do not check your brain at the door. But you make a decision, you align, and you move forward. The only reason to have a strategy and a product is to bring together people and enable them to success.

You can structure the conversation. **You cannot control people but you can control the conversation**—you can specify that this is about fact gathering or about making decisions. You influence very quickly the rest of the organization as people are watching. You create the structure, together the team delivers the results.

We've already spoken earlier about Shahan Nazar, senior vice president of product development for Estée Lauder Companies. He's the guy who led the effort to successfully integrate the Estée Lauder/MAC merger in R&D. He brought two cultures together to build a common identity. Nazar is a master at bringing people and teams together. He observes:

Without a leader you cannot succeed. Collectivism is a nice concept but it does not work. The success of a leader goes to maturing the team and gaining consensus—the majority must rule. But if the minority is not heard, the ruling proposal collapses. You must listen to objections and meet them in some way. Communism collapsed because they did not listen to dissent. If it is just the leader, it can be brutal and collapse.

Good leaders make a consensus of the team; they do it with the input of the minority—they need to be heard on their key objections and brought on board.

Some dissenters you can never get on board; some you can never convince. You have to neutralize them, since, if you do not, they can be destructive. If you do nothing, it is a big mistake. You cannot have people undermining you. Napoleon thought he had delayed the Prussians; but one of his marshals betrayed him and allowed the Prussians to arrive in half the time. He could not sell his strategy to that marshal; he did not neutralize him.

To gain as much support as you can, the key is to translate your strategy and make sure people understand it and can see themselves in the picture. First, the strategy has to be wise and solid; if it is smoke and mirrors, it has no chance. If it is solid and doable and makes sense, it is not hard to sell. You must spend a lot of time coming up with a winning strategy, supported by intuition, facts, process—spend a lot of thinking on it. If the strategy is solid, it can still fail if the execution is not good. That is when communication is key. You can't afford to have a Chocolate Conversation. People need to understand what you want them to do and be given the freedom to express their concerns.

How to Know You're Having a Chocolate Conversation

Leaders try to come up with simple ideas to drive change all the time. "Customer experience" is a good example. For the past several years, companies have been grappling with "best customer experience" as a key goal. Yet, some of the leaders I've seen work on this have not made their companies any more appealing in the customer experience realm. As a result, they've suffered lost market share despite a lot of effort. The answer is where chocolate comes in.

I've used the Chocolate Conversation exercise in my own consulting practice for many years. We use this exercise whenever we begin a new group session with a client. The subject matter of the meeting varies—we could be talking about anything from strategy to post-merger integration or from leadership practice to innovation.

We open with the chocolate exercise that we spoke about in an earlier chapter. Start by asking a room full of executives to conjure up a picture in their minds when they hear the word "chocolate." They've all tasted some form of chocolate, haven't they? Most of the time, individuals look around the room at each other and then at us rather curiously—after all, asking about chocolate at the start of an important business meeting does raise a bit of concern about how the rest of the meeting will go. Aren't meeting facilitators supposed to begin by talking about the objectives for the meeting? Next, ask participants to write on a Post-it Note the picture that came into their mind when they heard the word "chocolate." After everyone writes something down, ask for a volunteer to read his Post-it. Once the members of the group read what is on their Post-it Notes, people begin smiling at each other, as we are connecting their words and playfully making commentary like, "You want strawberries dipped in chocolate, but this guy wants to make sure it's dark chocolate and this woman wants hot fudge over strawberry ice cream and two other people don't want any because they don't want it to show up on certain body parts."

Change the word "chocolate" into words like "innovation," "talent," "solution," "experience," or "customer," and every person can immediately see why personal interpretation leads to multiple understanding and standards, confusion and concern. After this exercise, the participants realize that everyone has people have a different picture in their heads of what the concept means to them. The moment we substitute words like "innovation" or "customer experience" for "chocolate," each person there begins to get the picture understand. The trick is to recognize Chocolate Conversations when the meeting is over and people are back at their everyday jobs.

I have used the chocolate exercise with a diverse group of clients, and I've been gratified to hear them adopt the phrase into their own vocabulary. I'll hear them talking among themselves six months or a year later and they'll pull up short and

say, "Wait, we're having a Chocolate Conversation." Then
they'll make sure everyone in the conversation is clearly seeing the same picture before they continue. In a sense, the term
and this behavior have become markers for executives we've
worked with who have really gotten something out of focusing
on the "conversation" and then have incorporated it into their
personal leadership practice.

Good Leaders Can Have Bad Conversations

Leaders of organizations and teams have all types of conversations privately and publicly: conversations for possibility,
commitment, action, and assessment. Preparing for these conversations is key to the success of an effective leader. For every
Tami Erwin and Shahan Nazar I have known, I have met three
executives who are crippled by their inability to have the conversations they need to have. They are smart, hardworking,
and dedicated—and they get the idea of Chocolate Conversations when I talk to them—but they find it hard to have the
conversations that are important for their businesses in a way
that creates action. They are good people who consistently
have bad conversations. Let's move on to our next chapter to
find out why this is so—and what you can do about it if it's
happening to you.

Why Do Good People Have Bad Conversations?

People follow leaders. They listen to their leaders and act accordingly. That is why you will hear me say that leadership happens in the conversation—I've said this so many times, it could be considered a mantra for me and for my clients. If that is so, why is it that well-respected leaders can have conversations that cause more harm than good?

There is a powerful real-life event that those of us who were watching the news at the time will never forget: the terrorist attack on the Israeli athletes at the 1972 Summer Olympics in Munich. This event tells us a lot about how a Chocolate Conversation around conflicted worldviews can lead to disastrous outcomes. The attack on the Israeli athletes was triggered by a conversation that Israeli and Palestinian leaders and their people have been having for decades, and it revolves around two seemingly irreconcilable points of view:

- *The Jewish people were without a homeland for centuries.* European Jews were promised a homeland in Palestine by the British during the First World War, but the promise was broken. After suffering unspeakable atrocities during the

Holocaust and with no country to call home, the Jewish people were granted a homeland: the State of Israel was created by a combination of a United Nations resolution and a declaration by the head of The World Zionist Organization, David Ben-Gurion, which effectively terminated the British Mandate for Palestine in May of 1948. The State of Israel was cut from the land inhabited by the Palestinians. The very next day, neighboring Arab states attacked Israel in support of the native Palestinians. Jews from every part of the world felt justified in doing anything they could to secure a safe homeland for themselves, their children, and the generations to come.

- *The Palestinians were promised their own country* when the British took over Palestine from the Turks after the First World War, but the promise was broken. Since 1948, they too have suffered, locked in a war for a homeland they feel was unjustly taken from them. They have felt justified in doing anything they could to secure a safe homeland for themselves, their children, and the generations to come.

On the surface, it seems that both the Palestinians and the Israelis have the same worldview: homeland, safety, peace. However, the conversation revolves around the proverbial rock and a hard place.

Here we have two groups of people who have experienced a trauma that has undermined their sense of "home" and "safety," and they want it back. A completely dispassionate observer might conclude that the two peoples are so close together in their worldviews that a little discussion over specifics (standards) should address their concerns and serve to solve any remaining difficulties.

However, the problems of the Middle East have devoured good intentions for well over a half century, and the strife shows no sign of abating for one crucial reason: although it appears that the two sides want the same thing, and it appears that dividing the land so that all could live in peace is a tenable solution, the "worldview" position of each nation calls for the elimination of the other.

While almost every president of the United States has spearheaded peace talks and conversations designed to bring peace to the Middle East—and there have been treaties with a number of Arab countries that surround Israel—there exists, to this day, a lack of trust and faith that the people of the region can coexist peacefully. Neither people trusts that the other wouldn't kill them, if given the chance—and they often do attack one another. Each time it happens, trust is eroded once again.

At the worldview level, in this case, there is mutual exclusivity—one side can get what it wants only if the other side is killed off. This conversation exists on the level of survival. When conversations exist on the level of survival, it is hard—if not impossible—to get agreement. Basic trust and safety have been violated. Unless there is a way of reestablishing trust and safety, you will not be able to move people past their basic survival issues to establish a worldview that works for both.

Our first challenge is to determine the level of the disagreement. To look at the Middle East example as a conflict over boundaries or who gets what town or village (standards) is to miss the point. Survival issues can cause people to become violent if they feel challenged beyond their tolerance.

There are plenty of examples in every sphere of life. For politicians, issues like Social Security and health care are battlegrounds for powerful constituencies who have different worldviews. These differences paralyze genuine open debate. Members of Congress might not say so, but I sense they approach issues like these with a "win/lose" attitude. In spite of the fact that they are members of a body that is entrusted to make the best decisions for the entire country, in reality, they pull only for their party's point of view and exclude the opposing party's point of view. This is what has polarized the political debate in our country for years now.

Business leaders face the same problems as they grapple with issues like spiraling pension liabilities and runaway health-care costs. These issues are topics in union negotiations, where Chocolate Conversations go on for weeks and months and sometimes longer. Both parties recognize that rising costs are forcing changes in employee benefits. Employees realize that everything costs more. It's a double-edged sword. Rising costs support the rationale that companies can't afford to contribute more to employee benefits; the companies' very survival is at stake if it doesn't make cuts somewhere. To further exacerbate the debate, executive bonuses can be so high in those very same companies that it seems like an easy fix to use the bonuses to even out the gap. Needless to say, the executives who get those bonuses don't want to consider that option.

We have all witnessed large and small businesses reducing their workforce to accommodate rising costs. In these cases, the outcome is people losing their jobs, with the ones left behind having to do more with less. These problems aren't going away. Unions are fighting to survive in a pay-as-you-go economy, employees are fighting to keep their jobs, and companies are fighting to stay in business.

So, why can't smart people get in a room, have the tough conversations, and work to find a solution? It requires that each party agree on a common worldview and establish new standards everyone can live by. Leaders have to break through the stalemate by pushing through the mutually exclusive, "you win, I lose" scenario and arriving at a point where everyone can make a contribution. So how do you negotiate a win-win in these situations? It helps to start with the concerns. If you can get people's fears out on the table and address them, you can do a bottoms-up negotiation to the standards that would help alleviate the concerns. Lastly you can validate your common worldview. Reversing the order helps move through the stalemate.

What You Say and How
You Say It Matters

As we've discussed in earlier chapters, the biggest problem arises when people think they have communicated but the message hasn't made it through. The gulf widens when what you expect and what other people think you want are different. How many times have you sent out a detailed communication only to get blank stares when you bring up topics you thought were clear?

Your employees would probably be just as baffled as you are if they realized they had missed something important. The problem is that you might not have given people the chance to really hear you. I've read dozens of books and articles on communication that talk about a "waterfall of messages"—the premise is, if you get your message positioned in the right channels it will flow downstream, giving everyone the information he needs to know. I love the watery image, but the waterfall idea is a myth. Something certainly flows downstream, but it isn't what you intended.

Corporate communication problems are more like the children's game of "telephone," in which one player whispers something to a second player, who whispers it to a third, and so on down the line until the last player reports what he heard. Everyone laughs because the message is ridiculously mangled by the time it gets to the end. Many adults are unaware of how frequently they continue to play this game in their business lives—and how hard it is to stop. The key is to see what happens in people's minds as they translate what they think they've heard.

Media companies are really good at this. They translate what they know or sense the customer wants and capture it with a slogan or a thirty-second visual that depicts a universal feeling or a mood. Remember that Wendy's ad campaign with the little old lady who asked, "Where's the beef?" It's one thing to say, "Gee, our hamburgers are really a lot better than Burger King's or McDonalds' burgers." It's another to come right out and say, "They don't deliver—we do" in a way so simple and memorable that it becomes iconic. With an ad like "Where's the beef?" you get the message right away. It makes you laugh. It sticks.

MasterCard's "Priceless" campaign does the same thing— everything you can buy with the card cost a little money here and a little money there, but the experience is *priceless.*

Verizon's "Can You Hear Me Now?" campaign is another example. Yes, it says, "Our network offers better coverage than theirs," but it says it in a way that gets to the heart of what we want from our cell phone service. The premise is basic: we want to hear the person on the other end of the phone wherever we are.

Dunkin' Donuts was taking a hit when Starbucks and other upscale, "cool" coffee spots came into existence. When the economy took a turn for the worse, Dunkin' Donuts turned to advertising agency Hill Holliday to help it get back its customers and attract new ones. Without saying its coffee was less expensive—and actually tastier—than the upscale coffees, Dunkin' Donuts positioned itself as the company that America wants in these trying times, offering good coffee at a fair price without the hoopla. The slogan—"America Runs on Dunkin'"—distilled a message people of all ages could relate to.

In each of these cases, people get it. The message enters common speech and popular culture. It does what *you* are trying to do as a leader—help your people get the picture immediately through simple, clear language.

Something very clever is going on here, and leaders can learn a lot about effective conversation from it. Wendy's, Verizon, MasterCard, and Dunkin' Donuts are all consciously creating standards in the minds of millions of customers. We've talked about worldviews, standards, and concerns throughout this book, but let's spell them out again quickly with these media examples fresh in our minds. Remember that:

- Worldviews are the beliefs that we hold about ourselves, others, and the world itself, based on our experiences. They shape the picture of reality we each carry around in our heads.
- Standards are the guidelines we have in our heads that direct how we act and evaluate what we see. They become our expectations.

Concerns arise in our minds based on the way we interpret worldviews and standards. When our expectations are not met we express our disappointment through concerns. A concern is an unmet need.

The common element in the media marketing messages is a clear link to a worldview—a good customer experience—and a product that delivers in a way that connects to the worldview. Listeners feel that Wendy's concerns are their concerns. They can see themselves in the MasterCard commercials, having those "priceless" experiences.

Throughout this book, I've been talking about how important it is to have your people see themselves in the change that has to happen in your company. Every one of these advertising campaigns is doing that very thing. Each is saying, "Change your behavior and make me your preferred provider because I offer an experience *that you **want**.*"

This is the same task you face as a leader: you must get employees to want to work for you because you and the company offer an experience they *want*. A company that does this well is Ralph Lauren. Their employees see and talk about the brand as though it were an extension of them. In essence, the brand is satisfying a need they have on either a conscious or on a subconscious level. A brand is a thought or a vision and when employees work for a company, it must excite that vision.

Like your customers, employees *want* to see themselves in that vision.

Ralph Lauren Companies is held up in the marketplace as the seamless example of creating a vision that their customers and employees live into. Ralph Lauren, the CEO, started with a vision of an upscale lifestyle, but not all of his products are luxury products. He carries everything from simple polo shirts with his polo-player logo and simple, well-made pants, to furniture, table-top items, linens, elegant gowns for women, and Purple Label suits and tuxedos for men. No matter what he is selling, everything about his advertising, his website, and his stores reflects upscale, under-stated elegance and creates images and a vision of that lifestyle. If we drill down to what his sales associates wear, how they are groomed, and what they say, these all support his vision. Lauren has created a vision with which his customers and employees align, and by delivering that vision time and time again, he has developed the greatest cross-channel brand in the fashion industry today.

What is as important is that his sales associates are so indoctrinated into the "Ralph Lauren culture," that their conversation is peppered with, "We recommend…" or "Ralph recommends wearing this jacket with that pant…" To speak with one of his employees is to be drawn into the Ralph Lauren vision—and, hence, the company message. By aligning with your employees in this way, your company becomes your targeted customers' company—you want them to see what's in it for them so "we" can transform "our" company.

Let's think about how companies develop their messages. I assure you, they do it carefully, because they have to be able to deliver on their promises. Like the Energizer Bunny, another great campaign, these companies need to live up to the standards they excite, and they have to keep going and going and going. When you reach out to your customers at this level, your message has to be the outward part of a conversation you are having with them. The beauty is that people on the inside are hearing what your customers are hearing and everyone is on the same page.

The Conversation on the Inside Ought to Mirror the Conversation on the Outside

When our firm started working with Verizon Wireless, the company's network message, "Can you hear me now?," was the rallying cry throughout the organization at all levels. Everyone from leaders to frontline employees beamed with pride that their company was the preferred carrier that delivered on its promise every day.

I remember having an interview with the chief technology officer. I asked him what was top of mind for him as a leader. His response caught me off guard. I am rarely surprised by a leader's response, but this one stuck with me. He said, "Every day, I wake up in the morning with one focus: we have to deliver on the promise of our advertising." That impressed me. Here was a leader who was bringing the conversation the company was having with its customers to his engineers every day.

Here's a story I heard secondhand while working with media firms in a large marketing communications holding firm:

A number of years ago, UPS invited a number of advertising executives into their office to discuss a new advertising campaign for the company. The various pitches from the ad folks were all falling flat for the assembled UPS senior leaders. Pitch after pitch landed to silence in the room until one of the UPS leaders got tired of it all. He demanded to know why the ad people weren't coming up with anything that captured the essence of UPS. "What are we supposed to do?" one of the ad people said, "You're a brown company." "Oh really?" the UPS leader shot back. "Well, let me tell you what this brown company can do for you!"

This executive passionately laid out what UPS was really about: the strong identity, the commitment to quality, its dependability, its strong sense of accountability, and a lot of pride, right down to the distinctive *brown* trucks. His colleagues were as engaged as he was, nodding and leaning into the presentation—they were in the conversation with him as if they were all one. At the end, they collectively leaned across the table as the UPS leader slapped his hand on the table for emphasis and shouted, "And that's what brown can do for you!"

The ad agency people had the good sense to realize that they had just heard an authentic, passionate message from the "inside" of UPS, voiced through its equally committed and passionate leader. This was the conversation they could and should have with customers on the outside. "What can brown do for you?" is yet another iconic message, intimately tied to the conversation within the company. Inherent in the slogan is the core message: Here we are, an everyday business comprised of everyday people doing an extraordinary job for you anywhere in the world.

A savvy media company executive once told me that a successful marketing message is nothing more than "an obvious message expressed in a simple way." That is *exactly* what you need to do as a leader—and it's hard. Leaders are tasked with translating complex concepts into tangible and doable actions. The simpler the language and the shorter the message, the easier it is for people to understand and not misinterpret. This takes time and effort.

There are different conversations that leaders need to have to convey their messages. We've broken them down into seven types of conversations that must:

1. Drive performance
2. Sell an idea
3. Change someone's mind

4. Share information
5. Resolve a problem
6. Recognize performance
7. Correct performance

There is a framework we use with our clients that helps identify the type of conversation you want to have and how to prepare to have it. It's a five-step method we call "The Intention/Impact Loop."

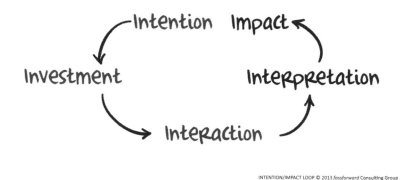

INTENTION/IMPACT LOOP © 2013 *fassforward* Consulting Group

Figure 5–1: The Intention/Impact Loop

1. Clearly understand your *intention*, what you want to get across.
2. Determine the *investment* in time and resources you need to achieve your desired outcome.
3. Determine the best way to have the *interaction*: public presentation, small groups, webinar, e-mail, one-on-one meeting, or phone call.
4. Consider how your audience will *interpret* your message.
5. Seek to understand the *impact* your message has when it reaches the receiver.

You control the first three steps and can only influence the last two. And the last two are crucial. Let's look at two examples of conversations through this framework:

Several years ago, I was asked to onboard a new leader who reported to the chief operating officer of the company. He inherited a business that was underperforming, and one of his biggest districts was at the bottom of the ranking. The manager of this district was never around when the leader reached out to him, and the leader was becoming more frustrated as time went on. This new leader never left work before nine o'clock at night and could not understand what he perceived as a total lack of urgency on the part of his district manager.

One evening, our new leader got home around eleven and went directly to bed, dog tired from a rough day. He woke up around two a.m., frustrated and angry, and fired off an e-mail to this district manager. The following day, the district manager forwarded this e-mail to the CEO of the company, asking if this was the kind of communication "leadership" should be sending at two o'clock in the morning. The DM went on to ask if the tone, language, and overall message were in keeping with the company's values, which he listed. He went on to say that his wife was having a difficult pregnancy and he needed to pick up their son from school at three o'clock every afternoon and drop him at home. He couldn't work late, as he needed to be home to feed his son and get him to bed so his wife could rest. He acknowledged that the performance of his district was suffering.

The intention of the new executive's e-mail was to communicate a concern and get this DM back on track. I took this new leader through the Intention/Impact Loop and asked some questions:

Given your **intention,** how much time did you **invest** in considering what method of **interaction** would best suit the situation? Did you consider how your DM would **interpret** your e-mail? Did you think your e-mail would achieve your desired outcome? What **impact** did your e-mail have on your DM and ultimately on you?

This new leader learned a painful lesson that a simple pause before he hit the send button could have prevented. The criticality of the performance challenge warranted a face-to-face meeting with this DM. That conversation would have uncovered the worldviews, standards, and concerns of both parties. This leader, with the help of his Human Resources partner, granted his district manager a family leave of absence and put a high-potential candidate in the interim position until the regular DM returned to work. Performance improved and everyone got what he needed.

The second example is short and effective. We work with a high-energy, smart Human Resources executive, Martha Delehanty. She has oversight for Verizon Enterprise Solutions, Verizon Mass Markets, and Verizon Corporate Services. It's a big responsibility, which requires lots of domestic and global travel, long hours, and countless meetings. She and her HR leadership team are working 24–7 with their business leaders to provide the counsel, talent, and development required to drive performance.

It is difficult for Delehanty to touch everyone in her global HR organization as often as she would like. One day, I was sitting in a meeting when I noticed a young HR associate director smiling as she was reading something on her phone. At the break, I heard her telling a colleague about a text message she received from Delehanty. She had participated on a task force that solved a problem for the business. The text simply said "You rock!" This employee was excited to receive such a thoughtful text from the senior vice president of HR. She felt special and acknowledged—and, it showed.

Martha's *intention* was to recognize this employee and praise her performance. The *investment* in time was minimal and the method of the *interaction* was timely, contemporary, and spot on. There was only one way for this employee to *interpret* Martha's message and the *impact* was powerful.

Many leaders complain about their lack of time to interact with their teams and frontline employees. I ask you to consider that sometimes a simple message, delivered in a simple way, can accomplish more than a long e-mail, conference call, or face-to-face meeting.

Management by Meetings

Most companies try to get messages through to employees by calling meetings. I've suffered through my share of them, as I'm sure you have. These meetings are usually accompanied by several PowerPoint decks, which took people hours to prepare.

Meetings can take up 60 percent or more of a leader's time at all levels of an organization. Meetings are used for communicating, setting direction, evaluating alternatives, course correcting, and reporting results. A lot of executives we work with are up to their eyebrows in meetings. There is the weekly staff meeting followed several days later by the weekly conference call, soon to be updated in the monthly operations review. There are the meetings to prepare for executive reviews and board meetings.

Management by meetings makes it almost impossible to get things done and to move messages through the organization. People spend more time describing the work than actually doing it. I work with clients who literally spend the first half of the year preparing deckware and going to meetings. People get so bogged down in minutia that decision making slows to a crawl. In a surprisingly large number of meetings, the attitude is punitive—people are put on the defensive and just try to make it through without being called out or getting more action items.

When companies are not performing, the tendency is to

have more meetings. This impacts performance negatively. The more time leaders spend in meetings, the less time they have to work with their teams, solve problems, see customers, and drive performance. The emphasis shifts from an external focus on customers and market leadership to an internal focus on metrics and financials.

Alan Mulally, as the new CEO of Ford Motor Company, said after one week, "You have too many meetings. When do you have time to think about the customer?"[1]

Managing by meetings is not an effective method of advancing the business and moving people forward. When you are closeted in meetings all day, you risk losing your grasp on your business and your people. You are trapped by your meeting agendas. You aren't walking around the halls of your organization, and that is *precisely* where you find out what's really going on. Get out of the conference room and into the halls and talk to your people.

The meeting calendar is a shield that keeps us from having authentic conversations and creative moments. We find ourselves having conference calls on the way to work because the meeting calendar is longer than the workday. A client I work with said to me, when I discussed this with her, "Rose, I have no time to think."

The other performance killer is scripted messages. If you can't explain what you want people to do in a simple, straightforward way, you don't understand it either. Scripted messages sent out to many people beg for Chocolate Conversations. You have no idea how these scripted messages will "land" for each person they reach, because you are ignoring the "Intention/Impact Loop." And without knowing how these messages are interpreted, you will not know what actions they will provoke. They may not be the actions you expected or desired.

Scripted messages were introduced as a way to maintain consistency. It is okay to have three to five business goals written out so that you are clear about what you are all striving for.

Lowell McAdam, the Verizon CEO I spoke about earlier in the book, revised the corporate goals by putting them in simple, easy-to-understand language. One of his goals, which I listed earlier, was "Widen the revenue lead." Today that reads, "Grow revenue, it's everyone's job." This leaves little to no ambiguity, *and* he arrived at that simple message by having his teams work together to put it in a form everyone could understand. It's straight talk, and any leader can use it as a jumping-off point for an authentic conversation about what that means in your IT, Audit, HR, Legal, or Finance organization.

We've discussed the fact that business today leaves us no time to gather our thoughts and have authentic conversations. I've counseled a number of executives on this problem, and we've found a few key themes that help avoid conversations that go nowhere:

- Keep messages simple—express them in an obvious way.
- Walk the halls. Talk to people and test understanding. Be informal and helpful—no interrogations.
- Limit meetings. To determine which are necessary, ask yourself "Where's the beef?" Know what you need from a meeting—keep it short and crisp, and move on when you reach the meeting goal.
- Carve out unstructured thought time for yourself. Google does this for all its employees. Applications like YouTube have come out of unscripted, unstructured thought time.

Don't Get Sucked In

A conversation that goes nowhere often happens when you are sucked into the *wrong* conversation. This can happen with an employee, a peer, or a boss. It's a common pitfall, so let's talk about what it is and what you can do about it.

One of my clients, Jerry, was a newly appointed CEO of an agency within a publicly traded holding company. Jerry set up a meeting with the holding company's head of HR to discuss filling key positions on his team. These new appointments were part of his plan to shift the agency's focus and improve performance. He had already discussed the plan outline with the holding company's chair and board of directors and they were supportive.

Meanwhile, the head of HR had reviewed the CEO's plan, but had locked onto "improve performance" instead of the appointments to the new senior team. The moment the meeting started, the HR head fixed on "performance" and began grilling the new CEO on performance metrics and what he planned to do to enforce them. The CEO tried to counter by saying that he wanted to address the performance issue by filling key positions. HR thought the CEO was trying to sidestep the issue. HR said that if performance was the cause for concern, then they should stay on that topic.

The next forty minutes were spent in an uncomfortable conversation in which the CEO spent his time explaining the past performance of the agency he had been appointed to lead and turn around. The HR person, who was actually a lower-ranking executive, had co-opted the conversation. Jerry initiated the meeting with one agenda and the HR executive hijacked the conversation and took it off course.

Jerry confided to me that he didn't feel like a CEO by the end of the meeting. He could not understand how the conversation had gotten derailed so quickly.

Well-meaning, good people can easily get sucked into conversations they never intended to have. It happens all the time. How could a conversation like this have been avoided?

I had interacted with the HR executive, who was also relatively new to the holding company. He came from a traditional Fortune 100 company where HR wielded a lot of power. In the holding company, HR had more of an executive recruiter role. In agencies, talent is the product. Both executives were firmly committed to the success of their company and both were well regarded.

Sometimes it truly does begin with a simple misunderstanding. Just as you have a desire to tell someone something, he has a desire to hear something—but they may be two different things. The CEO in the example above wanted to talk about hiring people, and the head of HR was concerned about performance. You can see how the misunderstanding occurred. This is *not* the conversation the CEO wanted to have, but he couldn't seem to redirect it.

In fact, as he tried to change course, the head of HR became even more entrenched in his point. Why wouldn't he let the CEO control the dialogue? The CEO had initiated the meeting—it was his to control. In this case, it seems that HR felt that the CEO's reluctance to have the performance conversation was concealing a hidden agenda, a desire to hide something, or a threat. The CEO's attempt to put the conversation back on course was his way of reestablishing the reason he called the meeting. Neither one of them was satisfied with the direction of the conversation, and the CEO became frustrated by his inability to steer it toward what he wanted to discuss.

This was the counsel I gave the CEO: write the head of HR an e-mail and copy your boss, the chairman. I told him to state his intentions:

- Be clear that you are enlisting HR's support in filling the key positions on your team.
- Give the HR head a list of names you want vetted.
- Provide a deadline for when you want these positions filled.
- Let him know that you are available to discuss potential candidates.

- Say that you look forward to partnering with him to build your team.
- End of conversation.

I also advised him, "If you receive an e-mail response regarding performance, ask him to please discuss any past performance issues with the chairman. How the agency performed prior to you coming on board is not something you are focused on right now. Reiterate your request to have potential candidates vetted and restate your deadline for filling key positions." The important message to my client is that he allowed HR to co-opt this conversation.

Whenever you set up a conversation, it is your responsibility to set context for the topic before you jump in. In this case, when the conversation went off topic, the CEO needed to stop the conversation and clearly state that he did not call the meeting to discuss the past performance of the agency. That conversation had already taken place with the chairman and the board of directors. In fact, that was why he was put in the role. He was also cleared to fill key positions and he was there with HR to make that happen.

Reframing the Conversation

Another way to avoid being sucked into a conversation you don't want to have is to reframe it. I had that opportunity early in my career when I returned to work after the birth of my son. A woman at my office had a reputation for raining on everyone's parade. For some reason, she was put off when my coworkers began cooing over pictures of my new baby. She said, "Is that a picture of your adopted son?" I said yes, and she replied, "Well, there's nothing like having your own."

I could hear the sharp intake of breath from my colleagues in the room. They knew exactly what she meant, and everyone was appalled that she would come right out and say this to my face.

I know that everyone expected me to say something to her, offer some choice words as a comeback, but I wasn't going to sink to that level. I was so enthusiastic about my baby son that I took a moment to compose myself and said, "I know exactly what you mean. When my brother's daughter was born, I was so excited. I held my niece in my arms and felt so much love for her. I couldn't imagine having a richer experience. Now I have my own child. When I held my son—my child—there wasn't a doubt in my mind. You are absolutely right, there is no feeling that compares with holding your own child." There was a collective sigh of relief in the room. My coworker quietly headed back to her office.

A few days later, she came into my office and apologized for what she had said. After she thought about it, she realized that, for whatever reason, she was being mean-spirited. She was so surprised by my response that she began thinking about her behavior. She wound up asking for my help so that she could recognize that the good fortune of another in no way diminished her accomplishments. She was uncomfortable, but, out of my refusal to be dragged into a conversation I was not going to have, we developed a better relationship.

Remember that the conversations you have are really about the conversations *you want to have.* You have the opportunity to reframe the conversation, redirect people, and take them where you want them to go.

Leadership is a conversation. Think about what it means for you as a leader to lose control of your own conversation. When you get sucked in to other people's conversations, you have stopped leading. *You* are being led by *their* agenda.

Don't be afraid to remind people that you're having a specific conversation about a topic you need to discuss. If they try to draw you into another conversation, they are really trying to impose their agenda on your time. Be respectful but firm on this point. You can address their issues at an appropriate time. Continue to hold firm on what you need to discuss.

This is a world away from leaving their concerns and needs unmet. Rather, it involves listening, forethought, and message discipline on your part. We've talked about these things separately throughout our conversation in this book. When you don't allow yourself to get sucked in, you get your message across and you are still addressing people's unmet needs. You are bringing together all the things we've talked about. You've moved from Chocolate Conversations to leadership conversations that can change everything about your business.

Keep in mind that you have the right to be prepared for these leadership conversations. Use preparation to avoid being sucked into conversations you don't want to have. Better to tell someone truthfully that you want to take the time to prepare a solid response to their concerns than to divulge information you wish you hadn't, commit yourself to something you didn't intend, or answer in a way others find flippant or inappropriate. Others will accept your right to prepare if you mean it when you say it. When you have to say it, say it.

In the next chapter, we'll take that point even further and look at times when you *must* say what is important to say to save your business, your company, your country, or, in the most extreme cases, to save lives. I really mean it when I say, "Let's *go there NOW!*"

Go There

We've all heard the expression, "Don't go there!" It crops up in movies and on TV, and, if you have kids, as I do, it's common in their speech. I hear it all the time as I listen in on conversations: "Oh, God! What if...?" says one woman at the table next to me at lunch. "Well, *don't* even go there...!" her companion replies.

What do people mean when they say, "Don't go there"? It can mean anything from "I don't want to talk about it" to "That's out of bounds." Even when people use the phrase in a casual or joking way, they're saying the conversation has to move on to another subject—the topic is just too risky. They're warning you that it's best not to know, or it's something not to even consider.

What people mean when they say "Don't go there" is: there is a background conversation that is off limits, either because it's too scary or it's too emotional or, in business, it's politically volatile to bring out into the open.

I don't know about you, but when someone tells me not to go there, I'm packed and ready to do just that. When I hear that expression, I want to say, "Please don't tell me where I can't go—I'm a big girl and I can handle it!" Once I know there's an "undiscussable" out there, I have to find out what it is—and why we're not supposed to be talking about it.

I'm not a fan of background conversations that never get addressed. Too often, those very discussions, if examined and defused, would open a clear space to address issues that otherwise stay unresolved. I can think of many "undiscussables" in our history that were harmful—even life-threatening— precisely because people didn't want to "go there." In business, I see this often; without fail, it is those background conversations that block the forward movement of the company.

Companies avoid "going there" more frequently than you would think. Topics that can't be discussed become the "eight-hundred-pound gorilla" on the meeting table whenever important company policy needs to be hammered out and new directives created, blocking open initiative and new avenues of exploration. Everyone knows this "gorilla" is sitting there, and yet people do everything they can to avoid mentioning it.

A number of years ago I worked with a publicly traded consumer products company at which a large ownership stake was controlled by a single extended family. The gorilla on *this* company's conference table was executive succession. Talent and performance would take executives only so far—once they made it to the level just below the CEO's senior team, they could go no further in the company. The CEO was a member of the controlling family, as were a couple of the board members. The CEO was finally forced to acknowledge the issue when executives with market-making talent kept leaving the company after they'd reached a certain level. The company couldn't sustain the brain drain.

Once I realized that executive succession—or the lack of it for everyone but the family—was *the* issue blocking vitality and growth at this company, I had some hard conversations with the CEO. I pointed out that losing important talent was the cause of the company's eroding position against more innovative competitors. It prompted him to have a conversation with other members of the controlling family, and they agreed to open the issue up for discussion.

So, how did the CEO get the gorilla *off* the table with the disenfranchised teams in the organization? He brought a large, stuffed gorilla—about three-and-a-half-feet tall, sitting down—and put it in the middle of the table during a meeting with business unit senior managers.

The meeting kicked off in normal fashion, with no mention of the unusual centerpiece. Incredibly, he got about halfway through the agenda before one participant said to the CEO, "Pat, I can't see you over this thing. Why is there a big, stuffed gorilla on the table?"

"I'm glad you asked, Cindy," the CEO said. "That's all the stuff—like executive succession—that we really need to talk about, and that never finds its way onto the agenda. It's been here so long, I figured we could just stick the gorilla there as a placeholder. We can even name it if you'd like. Of course, we can take the gorilla off the table if we can talk about things like succession."

The meeting was unlike any other the executives could remember. The discussion stimulated a huge outpouring of ideas about how to tackle the problem. The story made the rounds through the company in a few short hours, and the buzz was all good. People had been thinking about this issue for years. They needed a way to get past the block, and the CEO had to be open to a new possibility for his company. The stuffed gorilla signaled that the company was ready to address and solve previously undiscussable topics.

This company now keeps a supply of small stuffed gorillas on hand, and people point to a gorilla when conversations are getting too guarded. Pulling out a gorilla and setting it on the table is the sign that honest dealing with issues is getting off track. This is akin to saying, "Hold on, we're having a Chocolate Conversation." I like the use of metaphors to open up conversations like this. They are powerful yet lighthearted ways to help you "go there."

Earlier, we talked about what people mean when they say,

"Don't go there." They are letting you know that you are about to trigger something that causes them anxiety, anger, or some other profound discomfort. As a leader, you may find that *you* are the only one who can open up the conversation others are afraid to have. Let's take a look at what this means.

One of my former clients was a stickler for detail. He prided himself on being able to spot a typo in a document. He could tell the difference between an en dash and an em dash at one hundred paces. In other words, he could tell the difference between this – and this—. And that became what he focused on.

I appreciated that he had a sharp eye for detail, but he was hyperfocused on minutiae every time he had something to discuss, and it kept derailing conversations. These small typos, invisible to others, undermined his confidence in the document as a whole. The content of the document—in this case, a report on due diligence preceding a $500 million acquisition— became secondary to this guy's visual trigger.

People have verbal and visual triggers. Understanding them is the first step in being able to uncover an undiscussable topic and move things forward.

For my detail-obsessed client, the focus on typographical minutiae turned out to be a proxy for unease about being called out on figures. It took a hard conversation with him to get to his underlying concern: he felt that if his team had not properly proofed their draft before showing it to him, the *numbers* in the draft might also be inaccurate. In other words, my client did not trust the accuracy of the facts and figures in the document because he saw the typos as careless mistakes and applied "carelessness" to the entire document.

This client's internal bar for accuracy was set so high that he didn't want to let anything out of his hands. When my partner and I interviewed his team, they told us they were fearful about bringing anything to him in draft form, as he could never get past the first typo. We suggested having an open dialogue about this issue, and they reticently agreed. They were afraid to "go there."

I asked my client if he would be willing to open the discussion with his team, assuring him that this was the only way to solve this gridlock and get the better outcome he desired. He asked me to facilitate the dialogue. I often find that an objective third party can expedite the discussion and keep it on track toward a solution.

When this executive was able to get his concern out in the open, the team understood why he was being so "picky." They reassured him that the facts and figures in the document were well researched and accurate. The typos were not an indication of sloppy staff work.

Once they all agreed on standards for a draft, they were able to move beyond the impasse. They created a standard that all could live with: accuracy on the facts and "roughly right" on the punctuation. This allowed his team to pull in all that could be known in a timely manner and get the information down on paper without having to sacrifice content for style. I told him, "Once you understand the substance of the content, it can be proofed and returned to you for a final edit." This guy's "roughly right" was still exacting, but an agreement on a new standard allowed him to get through a draft review without being triggered, and then derailed, by minutiae.

The takeaway from this example is: be willing to identify the triggers that get in the way, openly discuss them, and make it okay for you and your people to *go there* so all can advance the work.

Another key point is, don't lose sight of what you stand for. One of my clients early on was a manufacturing company that was eager to improve the quality of its products. It had established a series of metrics around ten different quality points. At the same time, one of the most important components of the company's reward system involved the number of units shipped within a few days of order, and that number was measured each month. Everyone stayed focused on that monthly speed-to-ship figure, because it came up on reviews every quarter.

The situation crossed into "don't go there" territory when the quality points started to become mutually exclusive with a quick speed-to-ship number. Sometimes, quality steps were skipped in favor of that shipping metric, but no one wanted to walk into an ops review and defend a lower speed-to-ship number because of quality. As a result, what the company stood for—quality—started to slip.

Every manager I spoke to about a lower speed-to-ship number—in order to regain the quality levels the CEO said he was committed to—was instantly out of the conversation. The assumption that the company would not tolerate this made even hearing about it taboo. In this instance, the trigger was coming from, and being reinforced by, the company.

Fixing the trigger meant changing metrics in a very public way, so the speed-to-ship trigger lost its potency. I pointed out to the CEO that it was important to identify what he and the company were committed to and then get his team on board with that. It was clear he wanted *both* quality and an excellent speed-to-ship number, but the message to his employees was weighted in favor of the shipping number because that's what they were rated on. By restating the importance of *both* quality standards and shipping standards, and creating review metrics for both, the CEO was able to bring the focus back in balance. Expectations on both metrics were clear and out in the open. Everyone could now get back on track.

In this case, we had to get both sides to agree to discuss something neither wanted to address. The senior team was uncomfortable about changing the metric because it meant explaining to the CEO what was going on and how he and they had inadvertently created the problem. The CEO didn't realize that this was the core of the problem—he just knew quality was down, and that was unacceptable to him.

This situation required what I refer to as *the artful conversation*. *The artful conversation* has three steps:

- *Have the conversation about the conversation:* "Larry we want to bring something to your attention that is negatively impacting our quality standards. Without intending to, we are contributing to the problem." This is where you create a context for the topic you want to address.
- *Get buy-in to continue:* "Can I give you the facts?"
- *State just the facts:* "Our reward system compensates people for low speed-to-ship numbers. In our attempt to significantly improve this metric, we're unintentionally encouraging the teams to achieve it at the expense of the other nine quality standards."

At this point, if you have a solution, say so: "We have a recommendation for resolving this issue and would like your input. Is this a good time to discuss it?" Or simply ask for an opportunity to discuss the issue further.

Remember: leadership happens in the conversation. Preparing for the hard conversations by creating context reduces the chances for having a Chocolate Conversation and allows you to move to a solution. You want to solve these issues early on, before they become a death knell for your company.

There is an old U.S. Army saying, "If it ain't broke, don't fix it." If you read World War II history, from which that expression comes, you'll find that it's really shorthand for, "Don't try to change what you don't have to because if you do, you may open a can of worms."

A lot of companies live by that credo. It is seductive for market leaders to look at their past success and become obsessively devoted to it. Once that happens to leaders or companies—and they lose their willingness to look at something new—the people in the company become afraid to speak up. That's when "Don't go there" becomes the order of the day. They'll follow an ill-directed leader down a path to oblivion rather than speak up and lose their jobs. Earlier in the book, we looked at examples of companies, like Kodak, that lost everything by staying on an outdated course while the market was changing around them. Paying attention to what's going on out there in the world is how companies stay ahead of the relevance curve. Sometimes, to get from where you are to where you need to be, *you have to go there*; you have to take the hard look, you have to make the difficult choice, you have to adjust in a changing world.

Going there often results in shaking things up. Successful market leaders like Apple do it all the time. Apple is often criticized by market analysts for introducing a new version of a product long before the previous version has shown any sign of faltering. Those analysts fear that Apple leaves too much business on the table; the truth is that Apple never sees the downside of the curve. It is always one step ahead and one new product further into the future. For Apple, the company credo is "newer, faster, better" and "watch out, 'cause here we come," and that keeps it consistently at the top of the curve. Apple rewards innovation and new thinking—it is always willing to go where no one else will.

For more conservative companies, riding on past success is easier than changing course. The people in those companies who attempt to push the envelope are few in number and are often outmaneuvered by those heavily vested in the status quo.

In which camp does your company fall?

History bears out that the ones who "go there" are the ones who make the big differences in the world. It is always easier to stay where you are, with your current way of doing things and your current way of being. Let's look at a few who, when the world said, "Don't go there," said, "Watch me!" and changed the world:

- Rosa Parks, a woman of color in the pre-civil rights era, refused to give up her seat on a bus to a white person. In a world of segregation and no civil rights for African Americans, Rosa Parks "went there" by sitting silently—and changed the course of the civil rights movement in the United States.

- Mohandas K. Gandhi championed the cause of Indian independence by going to London to sit down with British leaders, something his colleagues found impossible to do. His nonviolent stand for his country and its citizens changed the course of India's history.

- Winston Churchill was thwarted for years in his efforts to get Parliament to listen to what was going on in Nazi Germany and to the impact it would have on the prospects for peace. He was ignored, ridiculed, and ostracized, but he kept "buggering on." From our perspective today, it's a good thing he did. He is applauded by many as having saved civilization.

If You Don't Go There, Your Customers Will

When you start to talk about the need to transform your company, you *must* have a very clear awareness of the thing that makes you, *you*. It's the unique flavor of your organization that makes you different. Some of the elements of brand touch on it, but it's broader than that. It's what you stand for and who you are for your customers.

I've talked about Apple as a company that comes out with new products ahead of the curve. But what Apple really is, at its core, is a company that believes in the newest products and the newest designs—and its products flow out of that core commitment to innovation and design.

So, what about a company like Coca-Cola? An iconic brand, recognized around the globe for most of the twentieth century, its mainstay is its popular Coke beverage, which created the company and remains a best-selling product to this day.

How does the company stay ahead of the curve and continue to grow?

Coca-Cola had to learn the hard way that it is not simply a beverage company—it is part of the "family," a lesson its customers taught the company when it lost sight of that. Coca-Cola is not just about what is in the can.

In the 1980s, the Coca-Cola Company experienced pressure in U.S. markets from PepsiCo's product lines. Coca-Cola sought to get a leg up on Pepsi in 1985 by changing the signature taste of Coke. The "new" Coke was only on the market for seventy-seven days before a huge consumer backlash compelled the company to reinstate the old formula as "Coke Classic." Executives at Coca-Cola were inundated with letters from consumers that sounded as though a family member had died. The public reacted so strongly to the restoration of the old formula that after twelve weeks Coca-Cola outperformed Pepsi.

The whole event looks like a terrible misstep, at least in hindsight. Coca-Cola executives had run focus groups on the new flavor well in advance of launch and the new product *did* score higher in blind taste tests. However, in those same focus groups, data had surfaced about the "sacred cow" nature of the Coke brand to consumers. Why didn't they listen?

Either Coca-Cola executives didn't know—or they forgot—what the brand meant to its customers. In the competitive rush to get in front of PepsiCo, they got caught up in the heat of the moment and believed that the "new recipe" was the future for Coca-Cola.[1]

I want to touch on that for a moment. It's called *deal heat*. When the top leadership becomes committed to a new idea, it can take on a life of its own that pushes all other considerations out of view. Deal heat becomes a kind of blindness, a faulty worldview that skews the judgment of leadership.

Coke executives got caught up in deal heat and they couldn't recognize data that pointed to a flaw in the logic that said a new taste was needed. They would not go there. They were convinced they were on to The Next Big Thing, and they got so carried away that no one in the organization had the courage to point out that they weren't thinking about what Coke meant to customers. So, the customers had to tell them.

What they forgot is that Coke had been part of life for so many; it was often the first soda pop kids had, and adults enjoyed it at sports events and picnics or as a simple beverage with a meal. Customers looked at Coke as part of the family and social landscape.

The way Coke can, and did, grow is by watching the market for changes in consumer behavior and adding to its product line, not changing who it is. As consumers became more fitness and health conscious, Coke came to realize that its real competition wasn't PepsiCo, it was *water*. The company added the Dasani brand of water to compete in that marketplace without damaging customer loyalty for Coca-Cola.

At the end of the day, the common worldview of an organization has to be validated by market reality. You could say that, at one point in time, all of these worldviews reflected a market reality:

- We provide the best travel service at the best price: Pan Am
- We provide the best user interface in business computing: Wang Labs
- Consumers know we are the best value for their photo needs: Kodak
- The customer is king: Sears
- The firm led by Mr. Wall Street himself: Lehman Brothers
- The 28,000 percent growth stock: Countrywide Financial
- The business of America is General Motors: GM

Every one of these worldviews was once true—and then the market reality changed and no one inside the organization had the courage to point that out. It was too dangerous to go there.

Unfortunately, *not* going there—not addressing market environment changes or changes in consumer behavior, or even addressing the company's own internal change in focus—has led to the dissolution or near bankruptcy of these companies. If you don't go there and address the issues, your customers will—or they'll leave.

I saw this firsthand at Xerox. We had been a *customer-first* culture. Customers trusted us. We talked to them about what we were doing and engaged them in our new launches. Employees were encouraged to bring customer concerns out in the open. This was one of the first things we lost, and it did a lot of damage.

When we tried to change Xerox from a product company to a solutions company, we became internally focused. We stopped talking with our customers. Everyone in the company knew that we were losing our way. We hadn't connected the dots from where we started to where we wanted to go. People were afraid to speak up. I remember having a conversation with a finance executive I was close to on the team. I said, "We have a lot of meetings and we produce a lot of deckware, but do we ever talk to our customers anymore? Do they understand our message?" She said, "I agree, Rose, but we can't go there."

Every leader needs to go there in conversations with employees and customers. It's important to do it in a way that gets things out in the open so you get to a better outcome. This is especially important when your business is at stake. A look at the different fates of Blockbuster and Netflix shows both sides of this equation—one failed while the other went there and won its customers back.

In the video rental boom of the 1980s and 1990s, companies like Blockbuster grew explosively—it was a great niche for more than ten years, and Blockbuster dominated it. However, as I write this book, Blockbuster is bankrupt. When consumers first started renting videos in stores, Blockbuster's huge selection ensured that even the most popular titles were always in stock. Customers grumbled about late charges—it was the one thing most *didn't* like about their favorite video rental chain—but Blockbuster's sales were strong and its competition was weak. Let's face it, late fees were a profit center, and the company was lulled into thinking it didn't have to take the hit and deal with that one complaint.

If you don't go there, somebody else will. Netflix founder and CEO Reed Hastings recognized that he could build a profitable DVD rental model with no expensive stores and no late fees. Blockbuster's revenues fell sharply as soon as Netflix began nationwide operations.

Like Kodak, Blockbuster scrambled to compete with the new model, but it addressed the new model too late and with a poorly developed version of what its competitor already had. And top executives at Blockbuster remained unwilling to address the biggest customer complaint: late fees. Blockbuster still operated with the underlying assumption that "late fees won't drive customers away."

Employees heard this complaint from customers all the time. I was one of those customers. More than once, I asked several salespeople if late fees were a recurring complaint. One employee admitted to me that he and his colleagues regularly raised the issue with the company because so many people complained. No one listened.

Netflix was born out of what customers didn't like about Blockbuster. Customers didn't want to race back to the store to return a film. Paying a late fee on top of the trip added insult to injury.

As a result of customer complaints about Blockbuster's late fees, Netflix decided to charge a low, flat subscription fee, to operate through mail order, and to never charge a late fee— ever. Netflix saves the overhead that brick-and-mortar stores have by delivering directly to customers' mailboxes within forty-eight hours of a request. Customers were willing to wait a day or two to receive a movie in the mail rather than burn gas for the trip to and from the video store *and* have to deal with the hassle of late fees.

When you reach out to your potential customers and uncover their concerns, as Hastings did when he created Netflix, you can establish new standards. You will find that some things you *imagine* are deal breakers (like that customers have to wait a day or two to get their movie) are really *not* the customer standards of the moment. The standards Netflix was savvy enough to meet were *convenience* and *no late fees.*

When you understand why your competition won't "go there," you can find a winning strategy for yourself. Blockbuster assumed that being able to get the product right away was what customers valued most. That standard had changed over the years with higher gas prices and the financial tightening that most consumers were becoming sensitive to. Getting it fast—and spending more in the process—was not the standard that was important anymore.

Don't make assumptions. Understand what your customers care about. Find this out by talking to them. Listen to your employees. Read blogs. Ask customers what they think. Frustration over late fees and returns was not a secret. Blockbuster refused to "go there," and Netflix took advantage of that refusal and created an entire business on the back of Blockbuster's indifference to what mattered to their customers. A lot of companies won't go there, and it's a costly mistake.

Netflix was also smart enough to take advantage of Blockbuster's perceived ambivalence about the customer experience. As I said, the commotion over late fees was no secret. Neither was the fact that Blockbuster seemed to be ignoring this important communication, leaving customers angry and frustrated. So, Netflix again took advantage of its competitor's indifference and created a customer satisfaction campaign that put the "icing on the cake" in the battle for the movie-rental consumer.

Everybody with a Netflix account is familiar with the letter you get if anything goes wrong. Let's say that a film arrives that was damaged in shipment. You note this on the Netflix website, and within an hour you receive a note in your e-mail box apologizing and giving you a free rental or some other remunerative thank-you.

You must sustain that vigilance once you create or transform your company to ensure that you are maintaining the standards that your customer expects from you. As great as Netflix was at seizing the opportunity from under Blockbuster and making great strides in customer satisfaction, they were not immune to taking their eye off the ball and creating one of the biggest customer snafus of all time. Which brings us to our second lesson to learn from Netflix.

Even if you're a forward-looking company with great customer relations, a dedicated high performance workforce, and a killer app, you can still go off the rails very quickly. Netflix decided to split its streaming businesses and its DVD mail order rental businesses in two. The streaming business would be named *Qwikster* and it would be billed and managed separately. Customers could continue to belong to both *Qwikster* and traditional non-streaming Netflix, but there would be two fees totaling more than the old fee, and two websites, reflecting the two services.

Customers hated it! The move only served to confuse and disturb customers and investors. Netflix lost 800,000 subscribers in a single month during the promotional period for *Qwikster*. CEO Reed Hastings responded immediately by "going there" once again—but, this time, *perhaps* not enough. Rather than launch the new service, Hastings went into print apologizing to customers and saying, "It is clear that for many of our members two websites would make things more difficult, so we are going to keep Netflix as one place to go for streaming and DVDs. This means no change: one website, one account, one password...in other words, no Qwikster." While that announcement may have solved the confusion of two names and two websites, the higher price remained in place—and the company is still paying in loyalty and trust value for some hard feelings with customers who feel that the price increases—for no additional value—was unwarranted and unfair.

It seems that Netflix has weathered the storm—they remain the leader in the movie rental space. However, it has been a hard road to re-enroll some of those customers who felt the price hike was too much at one time. Netflix had good reasons to raise the price—they needed the additional revenue to stay competitive with their offering. Analysts pointed out that the company faced—and continues to face—escalating costs to acquire content for its digital streaming library. Hastings may have taken a lot of the bite out of the controversial move by removing the confusion, but the bottom line is, the price–hike stays.

Be willing to "go there." Stay in the conversation with your people and your customers. Have the tough conversations. Keep your worldview real and keep testing standards. That's what it takes to lead change, and that is also why it's bittersweet. You want to pick the right direction for your company, and the cost of being wrong is steep. If you have authentic conversations with your customers and your employees, you have the foundation for transforming your business. You can try new things and make mistakes, correct them, and stay relevant in a fast-changing world.

Message Discipline

When Alan Mulally left Boeing in 2006 to become CEO of Ford Motor Company, he was facing the biggest challenge of his life. He had turned Boeing around, and now he had an even bigger turnaround to accomplish at the beleaguered Ford Motor Company. Within two weeks of his arrival, he sent a letter to every employee in the company outlining what he was going to do and what he expected of every person at Ford. He told them about the business plan for the company, and stated:

Our plan will be built around three priorities:

PEOPLE: A skilled and motivated workforce.
PRODUCTS: Detailed customer knowledge and focus.
PRODUCTIVITY: A lean global enterprise.[1]

He had those three expectations printed on one side of a laminated card for all employees. On the other side were the words: "One Ford." Mulally knew what he wanted, and he made his expectations clear and simple for everyone.

In Mulally's drive to get Ford back on track, he challenged his team to revive the company's most familiar brand. In his own words:

I arrive here, and the first day I say, "Let's go look at the product lineup." And they lay it out, and I said, "Where's the Taurus?" They said, "Well, we killed it." I said, "What do you mean, you killed it?" "Well, we made a couple that looked like a football. They didn't sell very well, so we stopped it." "You stopped the Taurus?" I said. "How many billions of dollars does it cost to build brand loyalty around a name?" "Well, we thought it was so damaged that we named it the Five Hundred." I said, "Well, you've got until tomorrow to find a vehicle to put the Taurus name on because that's why I'm here. Then you have two years to make the coolest vehicle that you can possibly make." The 2010 Taurus is arriving on the market this spring, and while it is not as startling as the original 1986 Taurus, it is still pretty cool.[2]

Could anyone mistake what the CEO wanted after that?

At the core of everything a great leader does is *message discipline*. Iconic leaders make sure they have distilled what they want to a clear, concise message that all people understand—and then they drive it through to everyone in the company. In the case of Ford, Mulally's message was simple, clear, and inspiring—something everyone in the company could line up behind.

Clear the Clutter

When Steve Jobs came back to Apple with the acquisition of NeXT, he saw immediately that the brand had lost direction. The engineers were inundated with projects. The product line was all over the board, giving a confusing company message to customers. Jobs streamlined the product line and the direction. He simply said, "Stop everything you are doing. We are going to make four products: two desktop computers and two portable computers, one for professional and the other for personal use." He also told his team that these computers had to be the newest and most beautifully designed. He was going to make Apple the computer you "had to have." To this day, people line up for Apple product launches so they can be the first to own the most forward-looking technology products on the market.

Jack Welch, the chairman and CEO of General Electric, told his leaders, "When you take over a business, you have three options: Fix it, sell it, or close it." No ambiguity there: his leaders knew exactly what was expected of them. Sure, there is complexity in implementing the direction, but there is no misunderstanding about what is required.

Successful leaders instinctively know that the secret to running a successful business is *message discipline*. It is my firm belief that *message discipline drives operational discipline*. I've often told my clients, "People will do what's expected of them when they understand what you want them to do."

We've talked about worldviews, standards, and concerns and the role they play in how people get—or miss—the messages you're trying to convey. A lot of us worry that if our message sounds too simple, it may not give an accurate picture of what it will take to make something happen. This is particularly true in multibillion-dollar publicly traded corporations where leaders need to communicate with tens of thousands of employees.

Large businesses are, by nature, complex. The complexity is driven by multiple functions and departments that are required to deliver against objectives that do not always seem to be in sync across the business: the Sales Division has revenue-growth goals and Finance wants the revenue, but the Finance Department's priority is the margin. Each department may have a different standard by which it is hearing the conversation. It is important for leaders to "speak into the listening" of each of the business functions or departments.

I like how Alan Mulally makes sure his message is disseminated through the ranks. He has a business plan review, a meeting with his direct reports that is held every Thursday morning at eight o'clock. When he first arrived at Ford, there were departments, like Human Resources, that weren't included in senior-level meetings. Mulally changed that, so the Thursday meetings included every functional discipline, because, as he said, "Everybody in this place had to be involved and had to know everything."[3]

When that meeting is done and Mulally is sure that everyone understands his message—and that they each understand the others' responsibility in getting the job done—the senior managers go off to have their own meetings with their departments, ensuring that the message from the top is transmitted throughout the departments in a way that makes sense to them.

Once your message is clear, everything must support your message—every conversation you have, everything you do. In essence, you are branding and marketing your message with your words and with your actions.

John was the chief executive officer of a company that acquired another business of equal size. The idea was to gain complementary product lines and access to a broader customer base. John was actively trying to make a place in the new company for several of the top executives from the acquired company—retaining this talent was a key benefit of the merger.

The position of chief operating officer in the new company was open. John publicly said that he wanted to table any discussion of who would fill the role so that the combined team could focus on integrating the two companies and develop their market strategy.

A few weeks later, John had a full-blown crisis on his hands. Three of his executives felt they were being tapped for the COO slot. Each conferred with the others, dropping hints that he had been selected, only to find that the other two felt similarly anointed.

When John was confronted by each of them individually, he was bewildered. The conversation went like this: "I understand that you are interested in the COO position but I haven't made my decision yet. You are in the running, but what gave you the impression that you had the job?" All three executives had the same response, "You did!"

After talking with John about this situation, I began to connect the dots as to how he ended up with this mess. He told me that he frequently rode up in the elevator with one or another of these executives. On occasion, they would chat in the elevator or on the walk to their offices. At different times, John made some encouraging remarks about the new management structure that he thought were pretty neutral.

As he recalled it for me, one of these executives had said to him on one of those elevator rides, "John, did you see the financial plan I put together?" His reply was, "Yes, Mark, and you did a really good job sizing up the business opportunity we have by consolidating two of our divisions. We'll save on cost. Thanks, I like that. That's the kind of thinking I'm looking for." He remembered similar conversations with the other two, as well. He thought they were neutral, but each executive left the elevator thinking he had received a nod for the top slot.

When John explained that it had not been his intention to signal that the COO position was decided, each one left his office feeling betrayed. One of them resigned over the misinterpretation.

John was stunned by what these executives inferred from his elevator comments. He told me, "I was just making casual conversation!"

Here's a principle I live by: once you are in a leadership position, there is no such thing as a casual conversation. When you lead an organization, everything you say and everything you do conveys a message—even if it's *not* the message you intended. George Bernard Shaw once said, "The single biggest problem in communication is the illusion that it has taken place." Communication is difficult in the best of times. It's almost impossible to get it right when you're caught off guard.

People read into everything that is said, and they can interpret the meaning incorrectly.

In John's case, his affable manner caused a crisis for the new company. The executive who left played a key role in the integration of the two companies. He was bitter, and his feelings were known to his direct reports and to people throughout his entire organization. His departure left a void in the company and confusion in its wake.

Bad news travels fast. The other two COO candidates became cautious and guarded around John. John had to rebuild trust with his remaining executives, in both his old company and in the newly acquired company.

John learned a painful lesson. Chocolate Conversations can happen when you least expect them, and they can damage your credibility. It's important to postpone conversations you are not prepared to have. If you are in an elevator or walking in a corridor and someone raises an issue or starts a dialogue, you must be careful. It's okay to say, "This sounds important. I don't want to give you a quick response. Please get some time on my calendar and let's give this the attention it deserves."

Death by PowerPoint

Several years ago, my partner, Gavin, and I were asked to sit through a cross–business unit meeting and capture the key points of several presentations. One presentation given by a senior vice president consisted of forty-six slides. I didn't have a clue what this guy was talking about until he got to slide forty-four. We sat through forty-three slides before the two big points of the presentation were shared:

- *Point one:* His division could offer a systems-integration solution to mid-volume businesses that was far less complex and time consuming than the one offered by the "Big Five" systems integrators.

- *Point two:* This point was actually a request to the audience. Audience members had the relationships in the mid-volume accounts that he and his team wanted access to. He asked to partner with them to identify prospects from which both business units could benefit.

The following day, I asked the group if they could tell us what they had heard. We got a host of different answers, none of which landed on the two big points our SVP was attempting to get across.

After we listened to everyone—and realized that no one got the message—we summarized his forty-six-slide presentation in one sentence and the group was blown away: "We are an alternative to big and painful system-integration efforts, and we need you to be our pitch candy." The room went silent for a few moments and then everyone started to laugh. Once the laughter died down, people began to see the absurdity of the presentation.

I'm not suggesting that anyone making an important presentation should get up and put two lines on a slide. What *is* true, however, is that complexity leads to unclear messages and leaves people with no direction for action—and that leads to an inability to execute.

What I *am* suggesting is this: the point of the message must be first and must be as clear and as distilled as you can make it. Then, substantiate with supporting data points—in this case, that the SVP's division would implement a simpler integration and that the two business units would identify prospects and make calls together.

Gavin, my partner, trained at a military academy. He often references the way military leaders cut through debate with clear, precise instructions. If you're fighting a battle, you don't have the luxury of long-winded, complicated speeches.

The military is the poster child for message discipline. There can be no ambiguity between orders and action. The idea is to make the line from A to B absolutely clear, no matter what mayhem is going on in the background.

General Patton is one of my favorite historical figures. During the European campaign in WWII, his beleaguered army asked, "Where are we going?" When Patton's chief of staff came to him with the question the soldiers wanted answered, Patton reportedly said, "Tell them we're going to Berlin to kill those sons of bitches." That simple, direct message reenergized Patton's troops and they followed him into battle.

Military personnel, politicians, marketers, advertisers, and effective company leaders use message discipline to urge people to make choices or to act in a certain way. The idea is to win a battle or an election, cause customers to fall in love with your brand, or get people to execute on your strategy. Leaders and influencers need people to follow their direction. Message discipline is the basis for action.

The Importance of Listening

A critical piece of *message discipline* is listening. You have to be sure that your message is landing with people the way you intended it to. If you listen, your people will tell you what's going on, what customers are saying, and what their colleagues are frustrated about. These are important conversations. Understanding employee and customer concerns will help you close the gap between strategy and execution. People need to *see* themselves in the picture. They want to know where the business is headed and how that impacts what they do every day.

Being intentional—and inclusive—when you send messages through the organization is essential. Lou Gerstner did this throughout his tenure with IBM. He wrote intentional e-mails that went to everyone in the company: "Dear Colleagues, today we have acquired Lotus Notes. This acquisition is part of our strategy to provide our customers with…"

Everything anyone needed to know about *who, what, when,* and *how* was in his messages to the organization. This discipline was a major factor in the success of the IBM transformation. People at all levels of the organization looked forward to these communications and they paid attention to them.

You *do* have to get ideas across clearly, listen to be sure your message lands the way you want it to, and get people to act.

Politicians are masters at doing just that: they use words (sound bites) to give meaning to their ideas and then "listen" by using opinion research—focus groups, surveys, and polls—to be sure that their message landed with their audience in a way that moves people to action. They want people to vote for them and they can only accomplish that if voters can see themselves in what the politicians are saying. Message discipline, in this case, leads to votes.

Opinion research was at one time only used in presidential, U.S. Senate, and gubernatorial races, but now it is common at all levels of government. Politicians at every level have learned that it isn't enough to convey their message in speeches; they must know how the message is perceived and if it was effective in moving voters to their side of the political spectrum.[4] Often, the results of a poll or focus group will tell a politician that a theme she wanted to use just didn't fit the circumstances, and she is able to drop the theme or make adjustments.[5] That's what happens when message discipline is used in a conscious and deliberate way to alleviate any ambiguity, focus the message, and get people to act.

If you use *message discipline* effectively, it will translate into *operational discipline*: what you talk about and what your people focus on will determine what happens.

Let's take a look at some specific things you can do to bring message discipline to your company. As we talk about examples, keep this in mind: *what you say* and *what gets heard* equals *what gets done.*

- **WHAT YOU SAY:** Craft your message carefully—distill it to its essence. There will be detail behind these messages, but first get the main idea across; consider, for example, Jack Welch's message that when you buy a company you have to, "Fix it, sell it, or close it." Be clear about what you expect and what you want people to do. Keep the language simple. Verbose language leads to confusion. If you are communicating to a large audience with multiple functions represented, make sure your function-specific message is heard by all members of your organization, but differentiate the specifics for that role. Ensure that all disciplines can see the role they play within the larger company model.
- **WHAT GETS HEARD:** Listen to your people. Seek feedback and do something with it. Be sensitive to what people are telling you. Understanding employee and customer concerns *closes the strategy execution gap.*
- **WHAT GETS DONE**: This is the action that is taken as a result of your message. Make sure that you—your leadership and everyone accountable—can see what is getting done, and that what people are doing lines up with your message.

Remember: *message discipline drives operational discipline.* Be brutally honest with yourself when you look at your results. If what is getting done is *not* aligned with the company direction, your message is not getting through to the organization. You own that! *Execution validates strategy.* Make sure it *is* clear and keep testing alignment.

It's All in the Context

Think about what happens when you meet a group of employees. You're going to tell them something about the business and what you need them to do. They have only a small piece of the context that you have. You know the whole thing. You have a lot of stuff to dump in their tiny frame of reference.

So, we have a communication gap here. There is risk of confusion and noise. You face what my partner refers to as "the curse of knowledge." Any time you know significantly more than your audience, you run the risk of assuming they know what you are talking about. That is often not the case.

If you are the top executive—or are on the executive leadership team—and you're in the midst of a company-wide transformation, you will know a lot more than most of the people in the company. Getting your message across to everyone requires time and preparation. At top levels of leadership, it is as important to be a *context* expert as it is to be a *content* expert. Just think of it as the difference between the forest and the trees. You're the one who can see the forest. They can only see their own tree. If you give people the backstory for how you came to the decisions and choices you've made, you will help them connect to the bigger picture. People need more context than most leaders provide.

This was a valuable lesson I learned while attending a leadership conference at MIT. I was asked to give a talk on leadership to a group of students. I was a little nervous about addressing this particular audience. Keenly aware that everyone accepted to MIT has a perfect SAT score and an off-the-charts IQ, I wondered, "What can they learn from me?"

The gentleman who asked me to speak, Dr. Kostenbaum, sensed that I wasn't my usual effervescent self. When I told him what was bothering me, he led me through a corridor into an area with an open archway. He asked me to read the inscription above the arch. It said, "If you can put what you know into a context, it's worth 80 IQ points."

Dr. Kostenbaum smiled at me and said, "You, my dear, are a context expert. Do not worry. You have a lot to offer these students." I went on to deliver my presentation and was pleasantly surprised at the warm and inquisitive reception I received from these young, brilliant students. This stuff isn't taught in most universities.

One of our clients, Martha Delehanty, handled the context challenge beautifully. She is the head of a large, global Human Resources team. Martha brought her team together to plan their strategy for the coming year. How did she get one hundred leaders and their local teams all working consistently in the same direction? She took a look at how HR's efforts fit into the company's strategy and she did a superb job of setting the context. She boiled it all down to a few simple goals.

This was the centerpiece of her strategy presentation:

To transform this company, we are going to have to bring new skill sets and experience to the business. Our current talent will need to be assessed and brought up to speed. We will need to acquire new talent where we don't have the skills and experience, and we need to continue to grow leaders for the future. Here are our three strategic goals we need to live by:

- Keep good people
- Get good people
- Grow good people

She detailed the specifics under each of these points. There was a lot to work out, considering there were different needs for different geographic regions. However, the basic mantra—Keep, Get, Grow—made it easy for this big group to work effectively. *How* they would make that happen and what it would look like became a story everyone was part of, built around a simple, clear, memorable message. And her people left the meeting with a very distinct idea of how they fit into the bigger picture and what their leader wanted them to do.

Here is another great example. A few years ago, Emilio Botin, the chairman of Banco Santander, spoke about how his company stayed the course during the financial services collapse of 2008. He had instilled three simple principles that his people lived by:

"If you don't fully understand an instrument, don't buy it.

If you will not buy for yourself a specific product, don't try to sell it.

If you don't know very well your customers, don't lend them any money."

Botin's message was clear, unambiguous, and powerful. He knew the context in which he and his bank executives were living, and he laid out a clear path forward. Everyone at Banco Santander knew exactly what their CEO stood for and what he expected of them.

Clear and Simple

In these stories, the leaders did a terrific job of communicating a simple, clear direction and staying the course. That is *message discipline* driving *operational discipline*. Let's take a closer look at how you can do this.

If everything is important then nothing is important. If everything is a priority then nothing is priority. You must be ruthless in your efforts to simplify your message to its core. This does not mean dumbing things down. We're not talking about shallow sound bites here. Every idea can be condensed to its essential meaning:

What do you need people to hear?

What do you want people to do?

What do you want people to remember?

Since it's so important to take complex concepts and make them clear and simple, let me define my terms clearly and simply. CLEAR means you are distilling what you're talking about to its essence. SIMPLE means using words and language an eight-year-old understands.

Bill McDermott, the co-CEO of SAP and the author of the foreword of this book, uses the phrase, "Keep it *Sesame Street* simple." That means use meaningful, single-syllable words— *keep*, *get*, *grow*—with no acronyms, no complex business speak, no corporate speak. Just simple, clear directives that emotionally connect people to what they have to do and why.

I and the *fassforward* team spend a surprising amount of time helping clients untangle the complexity they impose on themselves. They are so used to corporate speak and to concepts made to sound complex that they've become immune to it.

Cutting to the heart of the matter is always refreshing. It's not easy to do, but it's the only way to make your message heard the way you intended it to be heard.

Make It Personal

You want to say something that moves people and gets them to stop and think. Which of these would get you to sit up and take notice?

"A high closing ratio is a key factor in achieving your new business targets."

Or:

"Doesn't it make you furious when you give a presentation that knocks it out of the park and your prospect *still* won't buy from you?"

Remember, you're talking to people, not machines.

A client of ours is the SVP for Customer Service in a Fortune 100 consumer goods company. She was asked to speak to a large group of customer service reps from call centers around the country. The national target for churn was .08 percent and the actual result was 1.0 percent. They were missing their churn target by two-tenths of a percent, which was significant.

When this executive got up to speak, the customer service reps expected to see the usual slides with graphs showing the trends in *call-in rate*, *first call resolution*, and *churn*. Instead, her presentation went like this:

> Yesterday fifty thousand customers called in to our centers around the country. Seventeen thousand of them have been with us five years or longer. Sixty-eight hundred of them decided not to renew their contract with us. That was just one day. Every thirty seconds, we lose one of our customers. We need to take that personally!

People sat up and took notice. She made the statistics matter to them: no graphs, no corporate speak, just an honest, simple message that made the point!

You Are Your Message

Stay strongly focused on your message. You don't need to be a celebrity CEO to have message discipline work for you. Be clear about what you're asking your people to do. Keep a razor-sharp focus on that message. Don't cloud it with filler. And don't be afraid to make it personal.

Dale Carnegie said, "We are evaluated and classified by these four contacts: what we do, how we look, what we say, and how we say it." Part of staying focused on your message is remembering that *you and your message are one*. Your behaviors have to match your message. If they don't, your people will see the contrast between what you say and what you do. The result? They won't act the way you want them to. In fact, if your message is seriously out of sync with the way your people see you, you can do a lot more harm than good. Here's a perfect example:

In November of 2008, the CEOs of the Big Three U.S. automakers all went to Washington, D.C. They needed massive government help to avoid bankruptcy. All three CEOs were clear and simple. Each was in sync with the other. Each made a case for urgency. All said that thousands of American jobs hung in the balance. Yet, the three CEOs were slammed and ridiculed in every major news outlet and talk show for a solid week afterward.

Why?

Each had flown separately to D.C. from his big, fancy office on a luxurious corporate jet. Think of the missed opportunity! These guys are carmakers, but instead of driving their best product to Washington, they flew. And they didn't just fly, they flew like royalty—royalty begging the taxpayers for bailout money. Do you see the absurdity in the situation? The late-night talk show hosts did.

One of my clients demonstrated this "what gets said, heard, and done" principle during a presentation he was making on a new go-to-market model for his teams. He's the head of one of the major offices of a media company, and his teams were doing two things simultaneously:

1. They were coming together after a large merger for the first time, and
2. They were figuring out a new collaborative model of working.

Right in the middle of his presentation, a well-respected team member stood up and said the company's commission and bonus setup didn't take the new model into account. He said he had spoken to a finance person that very morning who confirmed that team members would actually lose money if they acted the way the new model urged.

My client enlisted that team member right then and there, inviting him to meetings with both the Finance and Legal departments to hammer out a new compensation model that complemented the new way of working. Before this executive left the meeting, he told the audience he would get back to them on changes to the compensation policy—and he gave them a time frame for when they could expect to hear from him.

These actions are right on target. This leader had been talking about collaboration. He immediately saw the problem his team member raised as an opportunity to model the right behavior. He suggested a way to solve the problem that worked for the group. There is no more powerful way of showing a group what you're talking about than demonstrating it in real time in a real situation.

Everything I've said in this chapter serves one straightforward aim: use message discipline to make things happen. Keep in mind the connection between what you say, what gets heard, and what gets done. Make it personal. Remember, people need to connect with you and your message. Otherwise, you can't expect your people to act and do what you expect them to.

Most leaders find it difficult to be everywhere they would like to be, delivering their message the way they want to. If they lead large organizations, they can't be face to face with all of the people who follow them. They need to touch people through multiple communication media: webinars, e-mail, company intranet, and presentations. All these communication media need to connect you and your message to your people—and they need to connect your people back to you. In our next chapter, we'll talk about how you as a leader can effectively extend your reach.

Extending Your Reach

Reaching your people on an emotional level is an indispensable part of leadership. It's the secret sauce that gets people to follow you, and—let's face it—you can't call yourself a leader if no one is following you. Some leaders have an intuitive feel for their people. Whether they are conscious of it or not, these leaders have a high emotional intelligence quotient. Others have to learn how to develop their emotional intelligence. The good news is that you can increase your emotional intelligence quotient.

Emotional intelligence is the ability to read people and situations. Leaders who have it know what to say and when to say it. They have the ability to kick someone in the butt when it's needed or put their arm around someone at just the right moment to restore that person's confidence.

Leaders who have high emotional intelligence get better results across the board. They are more successful at transforming their businesses and more successful at getting the best and the most out of the people who work for them.

There is often a misconception that leaders who have high levels of emotional intelligence are soft. To the contrary, Jack Welch, Lou Gerstner, and Steve Jobs all led best-in-class transformations and none of them would ever be labeled as soft.

Leaders with high emotional intelligence also know how to clear the clutter, and say things simply and directly. They don't have many Chocolate Conversations. When the occasional misunderstanding arises, they recognize it for what it is and they do something about it. These leaders know how to inspire others to embrace their worldview. They know how to be specific about standards, and are willing to face concerns head on.

The concept of emotional intelligence was first introduced to the mainstream in 1996, when Daniel Goleman authored the book *Emotional Intelligence: Why It Can Matter More Than IQ*, which became a popular read among businesspeople. For those who had emotional intelligence, the book gave language and validity to a phenomenon that had been difficult to describe. For those who didn't have it, *Emotional Intelligence* opened new territory for considering the concept and offered a framework for developing EQ.

What *is* important to know here is that having a high level of emotional intelligence will significantly extend your professional reach. Other leaders, community influencers, competitors, and potential partners want to be in the company of successful leaders. When you pick up the phone, the people you want to reach take the call.

My first assignment as chief transformation officer at Xerox was to onboard and advise the new CIO we hired. Pat Wallington was a high-profile CIO regarded as a strategic change agent among technology gurus, and she played a key role in the transformation of Xerox from copier company to technology solutions company. Pat was brought in to rebuild our global IT infrastructure, define and reengineer the business core processes, upgrade and consolidate our systems, and attract new talent.

A significant aspect of Wallington's strategy was to outsource the legacy systems, hardware, and services so the new infrastructure could be funded. Included in the deal were the employees who would transition with the legacy environment. We were in the process of approving a short list of companies for the outsourcing deal when our CEO, Paul Allaire, asked that IBM be included on the final list.

After an exhaustive evaluation, the team concluded that EDS was the leading candidate and best partner for the deal, and a meeting was arranged between Allaire and Les Alberthal, the CEO of EDS. Both men were awkward in the meeting, and the discomfort between the two was obvious. Wallington and our CFO tried to ease that discomfort by doing what they could to facilitate the discussion and summarize the key benefits of the deal.

A week later, Allaire met with Lou Gerstner, the CEO of IBM. Allaire personally met Gerstner in the reception area and walked with him to his office. I saw them walking and talking. Gerstner had his arm around Allaire, laughing and chatting with him like they were old friends. Allaire looked pleased with himself, like the proverbial cat that swallowed the canary.

EDS was the best option, hands down. It was willing to purchase Xerox's legacy and it was offering a large sum of upfront money that we could reinvest in the new infrastructure. IBM wasn't willing to do that. EDS had one of the best track records for managing a legacy environment. IBM didn't. In fact, people in the know at Xerox thought a deal with IBM would be akin to one lumbering elephant trying to tow another.

Meanwhile, Paul Allaire favored IBM from the start. Wallington and the CFO met with Allaire several times to extol the financial and operational benefits of EDS. Allaire talked about the importance of a strategic alliance with IBM. The decision was at a stalemate. They were having a classic Chocolate Conversation.

Pat and the CFO were missing what made IBM attractive to Allaire. It had nothing to do with financials and operational expertise. The attraction was Lou Gerstner. Gerstner was quickly becoming an internationally known celebrity CEO, while Les Alberthal was unknown outside the industry. Ironically, Alberthal was a lot like Allaire—introverted and a little stiff when you talked to him. On the other hand, Gerstner was animated, passionate, and a big piece of stuff, everything Allaire admired and wanted to be.

Looking at this from a different angle, it was easy for me to see what was going on. I shared my perspective with my colleagues on the senior team, telling them they needed to change the conversation they were having with Allaire. The talk track I suggested went like this:

> Paul, we get that it would be good for Xerox to have a strategic alliance with IBM. That said, we're not sure this is the right deal around which to form that alliance. If you do the deal with Lou, he'll know he has an admirer and a fan. On the flip side, if you do the deal with EDS, you've just made the decision Lou would make—and Lou will know he has a formidable peer.
>
> A partnership with Lou and IBM makes sense, but not for this particular deal. You might want to talk to Lou about going to market with him in other areas of business—ones where the partnership would be focused on new opportunities for growth rather than on our past and our old stuff.
>
> You might also consider whether you want Lou exposed to our legacy environment. It's pretty messy and fragmented and doesn't bode well for the new image we are trying to create.

That conversation won the day.

Both Pat and the CFO were intrigued by what they just heard from me. They asked me how I knew what was really going on. I took out a sheet of paper and drew three circles:

- The first circle represented the technical sphere: *What I know.*
- The second circle represented the social sphere: *Who I know.*

- The third circle represented the political sphere: *Who knows me*.

I said, "You guys were stuck in the technical sphere. You kept telling Paul what you know: the financial and operational benefits of the deal. Paul wants to *know* Lou Gerstner and he wants Lou to *know him*."

It was as simple as that. Allaire wanted to extend his reach by having a powerful influencer like Gerstner in his inner circle. He was willing to sacrifice the shorter-term financial gain for what he perceived to be a longer-term strategic gain. I told them, "By changing the conversation, you got underneath Paul's concern and you were able to support his worldview by giving him a new standard to have a strategic relationship with Lou. This required operating in all three spheres; technical, social, and political."

We will dive deeper into the spheres later in this chapter. You will learn a simple method for applying them to any situation where you are stuck.

I've coached hundreds of senior executives in the years since, and time and again I've seen them derailed because they are on the wrong stack of mail, just as my former colleagues were. I've seen talented individuals do excellent work and yet fail to advance their ideas or their careers beyond a certain level no matter how hard they try or how smart they are. I've also seen my share of executives—perhaps not quite as brilliant—rise and succeed to levels beyond their own and others' expectations. The executives who lost out are frustrated; they can't see why their talent goes unrecognized. What they can't see is that they are missing something vital to their success.

Why Not *Me?*

Let's look at the case of a client who had an opportunity for promotion in his organization a few years ago. He was an IT professional and had led one of the project groups at a large technology company for several years. The internal CIO position had opened up, and he felt he was a shoo-in for the job. He had a great reputation for getting complex projects done and he could rattle off important facts about every IT project in the company at the drop of a hat. He talked confidently with me about how I could help him once he was in the new job.

The next thing I heard, the guy was on the phone, bitterly disappointed. Someone else had gotten the promotion. The thing that hurt my client the most was that the new CIO was not as technically savvy. I could hear his anguish as he said, "I am excellent at what I do. I understand what is going on in IT at this company better than anybody. But some guy who is just a suit got the promotion. How could my company do such a thing?"

My IT client had the technical sphere nailed down, but he had missed the possibility that there could be a nontechnical side to qualifying for the job. The company wanted a CIO who had excellent relationships with the heads of the businesses and who could talk their language. The person they put in the job filled that bill. Technology partners were important to the company's business strategy. The new CIO had a large external network. He knew all the right people and they knew him.

There is actually a technical, social, and political component to just about every business situation. It doesn't matter if you are applying for a job or are implementing a strategy for a multibillion-dollar company: at every level of business, the technical, social, and political components are key parts of doing your job well. People who realize this and work effectively within all these spheres are highly successful. People who remain blind to them are often baffled when others who are less technically qualified move ahead of them—and they are left wondering why.

This was the case with my IT client. We began to work on his emotional intelligence using the spheres as a simple tool to expand his professional reach. Eighteen months later the CIO moved to another company and my client got the job.

Move Beyond Your Comfort Zone and Like It: You Are Good at This!

As we develop professionally and seek to advance our careers, we tend to rely on the areas in which we feel most comfortable. The way we lead—and the way others see us as leaders—reflects the areas where we feel strongest. These are where we are the most knowledgeable, the most confident, and where we think we look best in front of others.

Our areas of greatest strength tend to fall into one of three spheres: technical, social, or political. When someone else gets a promotion and you think you should have gotten it because you're perfect for the job, there is usually no mystery. It's most likely that the person who was promoted is strong in a different sphere than you are, and that is what is making the difference.

Here's how the spheres play out:

People with a strong functional talent and background may feel more comfortable trying to influence others by making a technical argument. This is where they feel most competent and confident. We tend to promote them into leadership positions because they are highly skilled, knowledgeable, and experienced—they have mastered the technical sphere, and the people they lead respect this. You can think of the technical sphere as *WHAT YOU KNOW.*

People in the technical sphere have strong subject matter expertise. They are great problem solvers. They know how to manage and get things done. They have a natural strength in managing tasks and projects end to end.

Some people are outstanding in the social sphere. They are excellent at bringing people together, building formal and informal networks, and relying on their relationships to influence and lead. They have technical expertise, but they are most recognized for using their social skills to make connections and secure resources outside their formal area of control. The social sphere is *WHO YOU KNOW.*

Leaders with strength in the social sphere exercise this ability beyond the basic building blocks of courtesy and respect. They are adept at developing and cultivating their influence in informal networks built on valuing relationships, at being available as a resource, and at collaborating and communicating.

Not everyone starts out with a facility for connecting with others outside their immediate circle. One way to get started is to offer your technical expertise to others. You can lead a special task force or join one. You can share a best practice or a solution you discovered with interested parties outside your circle.

When you're a leader, the job becomes less about doing things yourself and more about getting things done through others. Knowing how to tap into resources you need—but don't own—brings you the benefit of the social sphere. Becoming a well-known resource yourself is a stepping-stone to the next sphere.

People who are good at balancing the different realities in the company will excel at influencing others by supporting their positions and skillfully introducing alternatives. They are known by high-profile people in their company or in their larger network and are well regarded by others because of it. These people use their political savvy to drive agendas and bring others around. They are operating effectively in the political sphere, which is *WHO KNOWS YOU.*

The IT client I mentioned earlier operated almost entirely in the technical sphere. His problem was that his strength didn't extend into the other two spheres, and that was starting to impact his career. As he went further up the career ladder, he was required to influence peers in Marketing, Sales, and Finance. This required an ability to put what he knew into the context of those functions. This is often referred to as *socializing* an idea. My client wasn't practiced at this and unaware that he was missing a critical skill.

He is not the only one with this dilemma. The biggest blind spot many rising executives have is recognizing that their careers are about more than what they know.

If you reflect on your career over time, the technical sphere tends to be the primary area early in our working lives. It is where we establish credibility in our organization and begin to develop a reputation. If we mature beyond a primary reliance on the technical sphere, our reputations will eventually translate into a professional network and broader influence, and, eventually, competency in all three spheres.

When I talk to groups about the political sphere, I ask "Is 'political' a bad word?" Some will say "yes," and, clearly, a reliance on position or connections to give you authority might make you feared in the company, but it will never earn you respect and collegiality. On the other hand, someone who can connect all the dots and understand the company, the customers, the competition, and how to put things together and make things happen is a priceless resource and a huge help to others.

The political sphere is the center of gravity of the senior leader—the executive leader of other executives. Leaders who are strong in the political sphere have a stature and a presence that inspires others. They have an ability to understand nuance and overcome objections. They know instinctively how to position themselves and their ideas. They understand timing, that is, they know the best time to float an idea or bring a situation to the table. They see how to work in and around the system to get things accomplished. They manage upward beautifully and put everything they talk about in a wider context. Frequently, these are the hallmarks of leaders at the apex of their careers.

Each of us gravitates naturally toward one or two of the spheres, but to lead change and transform a business you have to be adept at operating in all three.

The technical sphere is where you have professional expertise. We spoke earlier about this sphere's importance early on in a career. It remains important when you reach a senior leadership position. People respect you for what you know and for "getting the job done." They need to feel confident that the person in charge knows the business and understands what's going on. Remember that this sphere is about what you know. To develop strength in this sphere, ask yourself the following questions:

- Have I laid out clear direction?
- Can I speak simply and informatively about the business and our challenges and opportunities?
- Can I answer the tough questions about our competition?

Getting other perspectives can help supply you with useful answers. Once you have this feedback, you can assess gaps and develop a plan for communicating decisions and actions you plan to take. As you improve transparency and visibility in the business over the course of several months, you will enhance your reputation and begin to show technical strength.

One client I worked with was promoted to president of a product division he knew very little about. He had outstanding business acumen and an amazing track record everywhere he went, but he was uncomfortable with his knowledge about the product line. He resolved to learn as much as possible in his first ninety days. I suggested that he ask around about product experts in his organization and tap several of them as tutors. He met with different experts on a regular basis for early morning coffee and learning sessions. These chats brought him up the curve a lot more quickly than just reading hundreds of decks, product descriptions, and reports would have.

The social sphere concerns your professional network and the influence you have. Bear in mind that "socializing" and "networking" are two very different activities (people who are not good at networking sometimes make this error). When you're good at networking, you can have a series of short, effective, business-focused conversations with any group of people. You become known for marshaling resources and getting others on board. Nurturing your network is important to you and enables you to enlist others when you need them. Remember that this sphere is about both what you know and who you know. To develop strength in this sphere, ask yourself the following questions:

- Who am I connected to?
- What are the strengths of my conversations?
- Am I having the right sort of conversations at the right time?

Making a simple chart may help you conceptualize this. Place yourself in the middle of a page. Put your boss (if you're the CEO, the board of directors is your boss) just above you and your team just below you. On the right, list all of your industry peers and partners, whether you know them well or not. On the left, list all the channels, departments, functions, and geographies in your company. What sort of relationships do you have with the leaders of these organizations and the key players on their teams? Below, list the community leaders who are influencers. Building your network means being able to have meaningful conversations with people in all of these categories. A good way to build your network is to talk with peers from other businesses and executives in the accounts you do business with. Ask them about the challenges they are facing and the opportunities they see. Offer your perspective. If you help someone else, she will view you as both a resource and as someone she would like to help in the future. This builds your network and increases your ability to reach resources outside your formal span of control.

As you get good at this, people in your network will call on you for help and you won't necessarily do the work yourself— you'll refer the person to someone else you know who can help him. Your knowledge of the corporate network and its various capabilities will become very valuable to others, meaning that you are now showing strength in the social sphere.

The political sphere refers to your professional standing and the power you have validated by who knows you. Getting a seat at the table allows you to influence game-changing policies and introduce alternative ideas. This is what you know, who you know, and who knows you. Think about this sphere in terms of the following questions:

- Do you make others look good?
- Are you furthering other agendas?
- What boards or external community groups are you a member of? These can include not-for-profit, artistic, or health-care institutions.

Referring to the chart you made to help you visualize building social strength, consider the names you placed above yours. This includes the company's leadership up to both the CEO and the board. What other top-level stakeholders are there in your organization? Do you have a parent company or venture capital investors? Are there shareholder groups or NGOs interested in your company's strategies and policies? Include all of these. Below your team, write in all the groups between you and the front line.

Because you have already plotted your peers and all the functions and geographies, you now have a diagram of exactly where you fit in the company. How are your words and actions furthering the agenda upward, downward, and on either side? How are you personally showing leadership in the eyes of all these groups? How are you a resource for others? How are you a champion for them? Answering these questions as you look at all the places you touch will help identify where you need to extend your professional reach.

Building strength in all three spheres will not only extend your professional reach, it also extends your leadership reach. It is challenging for a leader to touch everyone. When you are operating in all three spheres, your credibility, network, and influence can reach a large and diverse audience.

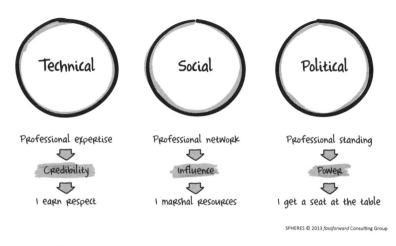

Figure 8–1: Spheres

Many of us are unaware of the spheres—we simply play to our strengths in every situation we encounter. But relying too heavily on one sphere has its dangers.

When you rely mostly on *your technical competencies*, you risk missing the political realities in your organization and you also leave necessary social networks undeveloped. People may view you as a content expert, but one who is not able to work the system. If people in your organization think of you as only a technical expert, they'll call on you to solve problems and love you for what you know, but it won't occur to them that you can do more. In a sense, you haven't shown them that you can. People simply won't think of you outside your area of public expertise.

You will also miss some of the vital messages percolating in your organization. Networks do something vital—they tell you more than official channels. They give you a context for why decisions have been made, for why some things work in the company and others don't, and for what is going on in the lives of the other people who make up your organization. E-mail and formal meetings don't give you the same background information that the informal network will.

When you put too much emphasis on cultivating social networks, people may see you as a "pleaser" who won't risk relationships over difficult decisions. No company is perfect, and there are instances of people who work their networks so effectively that they do get ahead—up to a point. The thing about most large companies is that, with each promotion, you become exponentially more visible, and if you don't have the expertise necessary for your job, people will notice.

In a senior role, you have to be able to make tough decisions or you will lose credibility with the CEO and other senior leaders. You also have to base your actions on a deep understanding of what the company does in the technical sense, or you will lose credibility with your team and with the workforce. Either way, your network will only carry you so far. You have to be a top performer and good at networking. Without the performance, people in your network will begin to feel that they are "carrying" you, and in today's environment that situation never lasts long.

Finally, when you put too much emphasis on posturing, position, and power, people see you as a "suit" and they discount your ability.

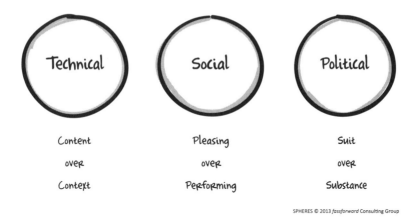

Figure 8–2: Perception of Others When One Sphere Is Overly Relied Upon

Facility in the social and political spheres requires an ability to read situations, understand what motivates people, and communicate at a very high level. This is where message discipline and emotional intelligence come together in the complete package to extend your reach effectively.

Let's move on to emotional intelligence and how it extends your reach as a leader.

A Practical Guide to Emotional Intelligence

A few years back, we got a call from an HR director at a large consumer products company. She wanted to talk to us about an executive named George. At the start of his career, George had been one of the company's best salespeople. He outperformed everyone on his team and consistently made quota in every metric.

George went on to run a sales team and again was in the

top 10 percent of his peers year after year. The team did exactly what George told them to do, and because he knew each sales rep's territory as well as the rep did, it was hard to argue with George's direction. The company promoted George to head of the Sales Department for its U.S. Northeast region.

It was a train wreck.

As soon as my partner and I talked to George and the members of his Northeast leadership team, the problem jumped out at us. George had taken over from a very popular leader named Paula, who seemed to have a magic touch with people. Everyone contrasted Paula's approachable, conversational style with George's formal, by-the-book manner. It was obvious that team members would go through a wall for Paula. They performed in spite of George, not because of him. We heard nothing but complaints about George: he was cold, he behaved as if no one could do anything right, he obsessed over plans and analysis. He couldn't simply talk with his people. Just about everything he said seemed wrong.

George knew he wasn't connecting with his people, but he didn't know why. He had always gotten ahead by using his analytical mind. He decided to try what had worked for him in the past—he called a meeting with the whole team and laid out his goals and objectives for the region, how he planned to achieve them, and what he needed from them. The team acted insulted, as if they'd been dragged to a remedial performance class. George knew his strategy didn't go as planned, but once again, he couldn't figure out what went wrong.

We asked George what he knew about emotional intelligence. We got an extraordinary answer. "I'm not going to spend my time talking about a lot of touchy-feely, personal stuff," George said, with the first real passion we'd seen. "And I'm not dragging my personal life into my job either. If that's what it takes, maybe I'm not cut out for this."

George's assumption about emotional intelligence—that

it's all about "soft, sensitive, private stuff"—is very common. We've met it before.

When you look at emotional intelligence as tapping into people and how they work, you find that it's got nothing to do with laying out your private life for all to see. Instead, think of yourself as a human engineer—someone with an essential business skill that drives performance. In the same way George needed to know what made his customers tick, he needed to know what would move his people.

There are several phrases we hear that describe people with emotional intelligence: "He's got a good gut"; "She can read the tea leaves"; "He can read between the lines." Here's a simple one we heard in one of our workshops: "It's how you *read the gauges* and *push the buttons.*" You have to understand where people are coming from—that's reading the gauges. Pushing the buttons is knowing what to say, how to say it, and when to say it. Does it sound hard to do? For some, it comes naturally; for others, it takes practice. One piece of advice that may help: trust your gut. Don't talk yourself out of what *feels* right—yes, what *feels* right.

Reading the gauges is the first step. Think of how many times you've heard someone say, "I just don't get this guy—I can't read him." If your team is a closed book to you, perhaps you are a closed book to them.

Read Your Own Gauges

Start by getting in touch with your emotional triggers. What sets you off? How can you use your emotional triggers instead of being used by them? What triggers you is one of your own personal gauges. It's important to become aware of your triggers because they tend to stop the forward action. Here's an example:

Renee was a senior executive who liked to brainstorm with her team before her presentations to her board. Her personal style was that of a storyteller—she presented facts with rich detail that contributed to the whole picture. After meeting with her team, she would send them off to prepare slides for her presentation. When the PowerPoint deck came back, she inevitably found that her team had cut out all the story and reduced her natural style to a series of bullet points.

Each time this happened, Renee would become angry and upset—it triggered her to see her holistic approach summarized in a few bullet points. She called me to complain that her team never seemed to understand what she wanted.

I talked to her team and found that they always left the brainstorming sessions unclear about what Renee wanted, so they culled her presentation down to its bare essence. When they brought it back to Renee, they were always surprised that she was angry and upset that the presentation wasn't the way she wanted it. This was a classic Chocolate Conversation.

In order to move the process forward—and to create a way for Renee and her team to communicate about the spirit of her presentations—I worked with Renee to uncover her trigger.

What she realized was that she felt personally diminished every time her team took what she considered to be her thorough synopsis of the business and reduced it to a few bullet points, as if *she* could be reduced to a few bullet points. She wanted the board to see her as a smart businessperson, capable of relating a context as well as the key points she needed to get across. Once she realized what triggered her, she was able to be clear with her team about what she wanted to convey and how she wanted it illustrated in her decks. She worked with them to create an outline and a slide-by-slide flow that would both tell her story and capture the key points. The team was relieved to finally have a handle on how to collaborate productively with her and deliver what she wanted.

Renee was mature enough to look at her own trigger as her gauge. Because she was willing to have the conversation with her people and work differently with them, she and her team were able move the work forward together.

How People See YOU

Another gauge is how people see you. For example:

One VP in an organization we were working with was a terrible project manager who blamed his people whenever something went wrong. He often referred to them as "clueless." And, he had no idea how his people felt about working for him. Among themselves they called him "Mr. Wonderful," which was a sarcastic code for "Mr. Disaster."

At a performance review with his boss, this executive was asked about the poor relationship between him and his team. "What are you talking about?" he asked. He was amazed at that statement. He responded, "They love me! I've heard that they even call me Mr. Wonderful!" With that, his boss realized how out of touch this executive was. That was the final straw that led to his termination.

You can't afford to be clueless, but you don't need to be a mind reader, either—you just need to pay attention. Here are a few things to bear in mind:

Nobody likes "perfect" people. What is worse, no one *trusts* perfect people. Someone who works at doing everything perfectly and not showing any chinks in his armor comes off as fake. It turns people off. We are all flawed—it's part of being human.

People are strongly attracted to someone who is unassuming and authentic. The paradox is that authenticity creates greater regard. It makes you real. It forges a connection with people. They feel comfortable around leaders who show their muddy shoes—and they'll be a lot more likely to come to you with theirs.

Don't rush to fix things. There's a big difference between being a strong leader and a "super-doer." Resist the urge to take over work you think you could do better. You're there to *guide* others—not to do their work for them. Your job is to set clear goals and objectives, clear the clutter, and manage toward desirable outcomes.

Take other views on board. Don't be closed to what your team has to say. Even when you have a very clear idea of what you want, talk *with* your team, not *at* them. You may be surprised by what they contribute. If you are closed to your team's input and don't actively enlist their collaboration, you may miss an opportunity. They may also take a page out of your book and work the same way—closed off and as if it's "every man for himself."

Seek out feedback. Let other people tell you from time to time how they feel about working for you. This will give you a reading for how you come across. You don't have to do this all the time—pick the occasions that make sense. When you seek this feedback, truly listen. Don't become defensive or push your own opinion.

Read Your People's Gauges

We worked with a CEO who had been the CFO before he took over his company. To say he was a numbers guy is the understatement of the year. He sounded like a math teacher every time he pulled his senior team together—he cited facts and figures, and completely turned everyone off. His slides looked like he put everything on his laptop into an Excel spreadsheet, and no one could make heads or tails of them.

This CEO succeeded in his career up to this point by always having the number. He found it hard to let go of what he was comfortable with, even though it did nothing to move the performance of his team. The CEO did not make it. The board recognized his financial talent, but saw that he lacked the ability to convey a bigger picture and take his company forward. The greater misfortune was that this CEO left the company perplexed and unable to concede that he had caused his own demise.

The flip side of this coin is a team we worked with that liked competing for stretch assignments. There was good-natured "one-upsmanship" on the team. The leader of this team knew what they were like, and she played on their competitive nature to step up performance. It worked because she could read her people. This approach would not produce the same result with every team. This team leader, unlike the fired CEO, knew that it's all about reading the gauges. Here are a few things to look for:

Different strokes for different folks. Your team is not you. What turns you on and off may not be what turns your people on and off. You may be the type of person who likes to know what's expected and when it's needed. Once you're clear on the expectation, you'll figure out what you need to do and how to do it. Someone else may want more detail and more face time. Others like to work independently but also like being in contact with the person they work for. They enjoy the relationship, but don't need a lot of oversight.

We use a tool called "Touch/Task" in our work that helps leaders get a sense of how to balance the relationship with an individual with the work you need the person to do. Reading the "how I like to interact with you" gauge is critical to making the tool work. Individuals on the team do a card sort where they stack rank in order of importance to what matters most to them in both touch and task. Touch referring to relationship and connection and task being about the work. Once leaders figure out the right balance between connecting with individuals and managing the work, they have far more effective interactions with their teams. The touch task tool comes in four varieties as seen in Figure 8-3.

Give them what they need to succeed. No matter what industry you're in, your team needs resources to do their job. They need tools and methods, the right level of guidance from you, and the time to do their work. In the real world, people always have to work around something that's

TOUCH/TASK GRID © 2013 *fassforward* Consulting Group

Figure 8–3: Touch/Task Tool

missing—insufficient information, time, or money, for example.

Good teams can handle pressure up to a point, but keep your eye on the "I'm being asked to do too much and we have too little to work with" gauge. When the needle on this gauge moves into the red, people will start to snap at one another, complain that not everyone is pulling their weight, and perhaps complain about you as well.

Read between the lines. Any experienced Wall Street hand will tell you that numbers are only part of the story. Read between the lines when you evaluate the performance of your people. How do they sound when you talk to them? What body language do they use? If you need to add another project this week or up the ante, will they slide up a notch and keep humming while they get the job done, or will they burst with the added strain? You need personal contact with your people to get a sense of whether this gauge is in the red.

Reading the gauges is vital, but it is only half the story. Armed with information, you need to push the right buttons— take your readings and change how your team sees you, works with you, and delivers the performance you need.

Push the Buttons

If your company or business could run smoothly and profitably every day of the week, you'd have a lot less to worry about. You're a leader precisely because business is complex, with many moving parts. There are multiple options and different levels of risk, depending on the course you take. Your team needs direction from you.

Everyone needs to pull together toward the goal. When you push the right buttons, you get everyone lined up behind you. This is at the core of what it means to be a leader. You deal with the conflicts, make direction clear, get commitment, and keep people focused on what's important.

The conflict: cool-it-down button. When people start to raise their voices, situations spiral rapidly out of control. This can happen in moments, face to face, or it can build in a slow burn over days in e-mails. The more people lock horns, the less the conflict is about the work.

Press the "cool-down" button by reframing the conversation. Take it out of the personal and back to the basic business problem. What unsatisfied need got this whole thing started? Be impartial, rational, and business focused. When tempers flare, be ready to press this button quickly.

The conflict: heat-it-up button. Is there ever a time to press the "heat-it-up" button? Absolutely. Posing a conflict can spark creativity, innovation, healthy competition, and performance. When your team seems to be lukewarm, you want to generate some heat. Be sure that you are reading your people's gauges when you press this button. Otherwise, your attempt may backfire and you'll need to cool it down again.

The simple button. If your people are locked up, overwhelmed, or don't know what to do next, press the "simple" button. Give them the three things they need to focus on. Keep the language simple and the message clear. Stop and check that everyone understands. Paint a picture for them and illustrate how they fit into that picture. People need to know what success looks like—show them. Give them a context in plain words. Make it simple so it sticks.

The commitment button. Walk the talk. Behave the way you want your team to behave. Work the way you want them to work. Treat customers the way you want your team to treat customers. Let others see you're totally in it with them.

Be authentic about this: people can smell an impostor. Appreciate others in public for their commitment. Use this button sparingly and for what's really important—if you go to the well on everything, your people will register high on the "commitment fatigue" gauge.

The motivate button. Everybody has a "motivate" button, but it's not the same for each person. Some are motivated by money—show them how they can earn more dollars and they'll take it up a notch. Others are motivated by acknowledgment—praise their work or accomplishments and they'll go to the wall for you. Some want to know how they can advance in their careers—knowing you are helping them achieve their career goals motivates them. It is important to have a handle on what matters to each person on your team. It will serve you as a leader and positively impact the performance of the team.

The step-out-of-character button. Many of us have a style that we are comfortable with and others are accustomed to. There are times when changing it up can be useful. Pushing the out-of-character button can change perspective, getting a different reaction and often a better result.

As a leader, you have to know what buttons to push, when to push them, and how to push them. One of our executive clients used this approach in meetings with his senior team. This guy had served a stretch in the military before launching his corporate career. He spoke his mind and had a clear voice that carried. When his meetings got off track, he would lower his voice and speak in a calm, low-key manner. Once the team picked up on the change in style, the room would suddenly get quiet—you could hear a pin drop.

He knew what they expected—he had read their gauges—and he knew what buttons to press to play it differently. By speaking in a different tone and volume, he stopped endless debate and got everyone focused. He was pressing both the cool-it-down and the step-out-of-character buttons. It took only a moment, and it was effective.

If you're a quiet, even-keeled leader, raising your voice and acting with a bit more fire would have the same effect. The key is knowing yourself, knowing your people, and pushing the right buttons.

Emotional intelligence plays a key role in our effectiveness as leaders, our influence on others, and our ability to get high performance from our teams. We work with leaders who do it well. For them, there is nothing artificial—it's a natural part of their leadership. It's not about being soft, it's about being practical and getting the job done.

For all who have struggled with this concept, remember, this is not exclusive to one type of person. You don't have to be an extrovert or love being around people to have emotional intelligence. There are leaders who have it who are more private and introverted.

Observe people you know who have high emotional intelligence. Watch how they read gauges and push buttons. Then take what you think would work for you and try it. Keep practicing. Tap into people on your team who have it. Where appropriate, ask if you're reading the gauge correctly. Remember, you don't have to be perfect, you just have to pay attention and be willing to keep at it.

Change Is Bittersweet

I pride myself in being a *change agent*. Yet when someone sits in my chair at the table, I immediately react by asking him to move. The truth is, I'm no different from anyone else—I like things the way they are. However, there is no growth in staying the same; there is no personal or professional development; there is no transformation. *"You're either growing or you're dying."* Nothing stays the same.

We can allow change to happen to us or we can take on transformation and grow into a new future. This is true whether the change is taking place in our business lives or our personal lives. If we don't actively take on change, it can come when we least expect it in the form of unexpected and, often, unwanted events—and most of us resist it when it comes. We all like things just as they are.

When my future husband and I were dating, we both had apartments on the Upper East Side of Manhattan. He lived in a one-bedroom walk-up apartment on Seventieth Street, and I lived on Seventy-Second Street in an alcove studio. There was a doorman at the front door at all times.

Once we got engaged, we started making plans for where we would live together. Because he had the larger apartment, we agreed to give his place a try.

It was time for me to move into his apartment just as he was leaving on a business trip. He told me to make myself at home, so I did. When he left, I brought some of my things over to the apartment and started to "make myself at home."

The first thing I noticed was the uncovered M&M candies in a bowl on his coffee table. After dumping them into a plastic baggie and cleaning the bowl, I replaced them with cellophane- and foil-wrapped Perugino soft-centered hard candies. After all, doesn't everyone know you don't put unwrapped candy into a bowl and expect your guests to dig in?

Feeling happy with my first change, I replaced a Lucite vase he had on his dining table with a beautiful crystal vase from my apartment. Moving right along, I noticed that the paper towels were on the holder the wrong way. My mother always taught me that you never put your paper products on the holder where you would pull from the top. It would cause you to pull too much at one time and be wasteful. I turned the roll so you could pull the paper towel off the rack from under the roll, *as it should be.*

Once I put a few pictures from my place around the apartment and some favorite books on his shelves, I was quite pleased with the way things looked. I had made myself at home.

I went back to my apartment and collapsed in front of the TV.

Ron returned from his business trip late on a Friday night, so we decided to get together the following afternoon. When I arrived at his apartment, I noticed the crystal vase had been replaced with his Lucite one. The paper towel roll was back on the holder the *WRONG* way, and my picture frames were moved. The straw that broke this camel's back was the M&M candies that were back in the bowl and my beautifully wrapped candy in the baggie on his kitchen counter. After I confronted him with, "What happened to 'make yourself at home'?" His response was, "I said you could make yourself at home but that didn't mean you could *change* anything!"

Thankfully, I had kept my apartment during our trial run.

We realized that it wasn't going to work for either one of us to move into the other's apartment. On some deep level, we knew that *changing* the *other's* space wasn't going to work— what we needed to do was to *transform* our lives together by *creating something new* that would be ours as a couple.

The fact is, *change creates opportunity*. If you're anything like me, when something changes, you probably feel disoriented and off-kilter. It takes a while to absorb the change and craft the transformation you want to see in order to create the new life, the new opportunity, the new business. I've told you of a personal transformation I created with my husband; here is one that a friend of mine created in her professional life:

My friend Kathy got laid off from her company as part of a sizable restructuring. She was devastated. After several tearful conversations, she confessed to me that she hadn't loved the atmosphere at work for some time. There had been so many rounds of layoffs that she had been living in fear of that next shoe dropping. Her company had gone through six rounds, and she fell victim to the last round.

Not too long after, she got a position with a start-up. Her energy and enthusiasm for her new company and for what she was doing were infectious. Her family told her she was fun to be around again.

When we reflected on the course of events leading up to and following her layoff, she said something I will never forget, "I got exactly what I needed. It just came in an ugly package." My friend reinvented herself and went on to achieve greater success.

Transformation and leadership require identifying the needed change, creating the vision, and executing the vision by gaining the commitment of all members of the team. If you don't identify the change that's needed, believe me, it will be thrust upon you. Leading through change is bitter-sweet because it's unfamiliar territory for everyone. You're the leader—it's up to you to lead your people through it.

Once you accept that change is bittersweet, you must

persevere when things get tough. Changing course when the road gets bumpy confuses people and slows down real transformation. Staying the course is the secret to most successful transformations.

There is a lot of misinterpretation of transformation and what it really means. Think of transformation as *transitioning an existing form to take a new action*. While the exact method of transformation may be different from one business to the next, *all* businesses must ask the following questions:

- What is the climate in which you're operating?
- What are your core assets?
- What are your barriers to success?
- What are your key differentiators? What is your competitive positioning?
- What are your resources and relationships?
- What are your strategic imperatives?
- What are your strategic options?
- What are your strategic shifts? What new actions do you want to take?

All of these assessments require that you have *deep, honest, raw conversations* with yourself and with your people so that you can get to the heart of the profound changes you need to make to transform your business. The answers may force you to rethink your worldview and establish new standards. These are the most important conversations you will have.

Throughout this book, I've isolated key components of business transformations and looked at relevant case studies to create a context for the change that is critical in every business. Now it's time to put it all together. I'd like to use an example of a business transformation that *fassforward* advised from initial vision through to implementation:

A colleague Gavin and I worked with at Gartner was hired by a global credit card company in 2002 to head its research group, which at the time was part of a newly formed Advisory Services Business unit. She introduced us to the president of the newly formed business unit. It was formed as a services business with an objective to advise banks and other financial institutions on their credit and debit card strategies. In order to create Global Advisory Services, the president brought in career consultants with financial services backgrounds to form a consulting group. From within the parent company, he added former bankers to head up geographic regions around the world. The third group he put into Global Advisory Services was the research group, which would take the company's data and turn it into research for Global Advisory Services' clients. Our former colleague was brought in to lead this last group.

When we met with the president, we understood quickly what he needed to accomplish and the challenges he was already facing. In his attempt to distinguish two of the three groups, the president used an internal naming convention that put the consultants and bankers at odds right off the bat: he named the consultants the *Big Opportunity Business group*—BOB and he named the regional presidents the *Business as Usual group*—BAU.

The career consultants viewed the career bankers, the regional presidents, as traditional in their thinking, and the bankers viewed the consultants as mavericks. The research group, which was neutral, had the intellectual property both groups needed to take to market. This research group often found itself mediating between the other two groups.

All of this conflict was further exacerbated by the parent company. Account executives in the parent company had previously given away data as the "pitch candy" to secure credit and debit card sales and promotions. The parent company executives and employees were not happy about losing this customer incentive.

Working with the president and his senior team across all groups, including the parent company, we successfully helped

Global Advisory Services launch and, over a one-year period, transform its business.

We proposed a three-pronged approach, one that we use in a number of engagements with our clients:

1. Take care of the conflict first: resolve cultural clashes and tensions of any kind, and get the leaders leading.
2. With the executive team, create an inspiring vision, one the entire team can get behind, and then evangelize throughout the organization.
3. Define and develop the strategy, the business model, and the implementation plan to bring the *vision to reality*.

For illustration purposes, I will take you through the process of the Global Advisory Services transformation.

Leading Change and Transforming Your Business

Day One: Uncovering Worldviews, Standards, and Concerns

First, we got all the issues out on the table. Our resident anthropologist, Susan Anderson, held a series of one-on-one conversations to uncover all the concerns. She spoke confidentially with all of the president's direct reports in Global Advisory Services, as well as with a cross section of the parent company. We prepared a themed synthesis of those conversations to bring to our first one-and-a-half-day interactive leadership workshop with the team.

We brought the three groups in and positioned them at round tables. Using tent cards, we assigned a cross section of leaders from each of the groups to each table.

The Chocolate Conversation exercise is always our first activity during workshops like this one. Opening with this exercise does two things: it breaks the ice in a lighthearted way *and* it shows that we interpret things differently. That sets up the context for the different points of view that each leader will uncover during the workshop.

The Chocolate Conversation exercise leads naturally into a discussion on worldviews, standards, and concerns as the three elements that create chocolate conversations in the first place.

Once we have that foundation laid, we open up *table talk:* We asked each table to discuss and capture on a flip chart how the way the three elements—worldviews, standards, and concerns—showed up in their interactions with one another.

We did the first report-out for everyone in the workshop. The issues that emerged were:

- The internal naming convention used to distinguish two of the three groups
- Conflicted worldviews about roles and responsibilities
- Different standards for engaging potential clients
- Concerns over the parent company's perceived lack of support

The Four Considerations of Business

We presented the four considerations of business: *relevance, growth, productivity,* and *scale.* After a brief discussion about these considerations, we paired people at the tables and passed out the synthesized feedback from the initial conversations along with yellow highlighters.

- Each pair selected one of the four considerations: relevance, growth, scale, or productivity. We asked them to review the synthesis and highlight what was helping and what was hurting the consideration they chose.
- The report-out was visually recorded by one of our graphic artists on a large roll of paper wrapped around the room.

Each pair did a wall-walk and captured on a notepad the illustrations that stood out the most for them. They brought their findings back to the table and put them on their flip charts.

✓ We asked them to put green coding labels next to the issues that they could do something about and red coding labels next to the ones that were not in their control.

✓ Lastly, we asked each table to put a second green dot on the issue that, if solved, would have the greatest impact on their success.

There were very few red dots. Most of the red dots that did show up had to do with the parent company's skepticism about the relevance of the new unit, its ability to generate a new revenue stream, or how they could scale their offering. We agreed to take the few red dots and address them in our Vision Strategy Workshop, planned for the following week.

We concluded day one with a summary of their output. The team was pleased with what they'd accomplished in one day.

One big plus that came out of the first day was a change to the naming convention of the two groups. The region presidents became Advisory Services Practice Leads and Subject Matter Experts. The consultants became Advisory Services Consulting. The name change dissolved the built-in conflict that arose from the naming convention. The new names clarified roles and helped distinguish the groups' responsibilities in client engagement.

The president hosted a team dinner that evening. The tension that had been evident prior to the workshop was noticeably absent in the evening.

Day Two

The team arrived fresh and ready to go in the morning. We immediately noticed a shift in energy—they were laughing and talking together and taking playful shots at one another.

Gavin and I knew that this signified *the beginnings of trust*, an important step in moving the venture forward.

We did a quick check-in with the teams. We asked each table to spend a few minutes discussing together the issue they had double green–dotted from the earlier session. We wanted them to take a fresh look. All teams agreed that the issue they had initially selected was still the one they would choose.

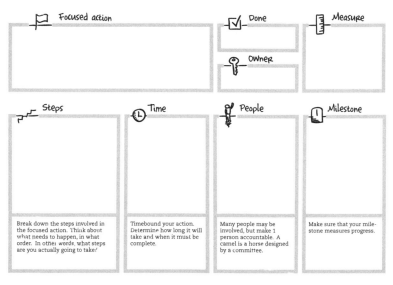

ACTION PLAN © 2013 *fassforward* Consulting Group

Figure 9–1: Action Plan

It was time to present our action plan process: each table went through the process of establishing their three focused actions and the steps to support them using the preceding action plan.

The Vision Strategy Workshop

Prior to the workshop, we had done one-on-one strategy reviews with each member of the leadership team. We used a tool, *the strategy canvas* to identify competitors and to assess where each leader ranked Advisory Services. In preparation for the workshop, we aggregated, by business group, each canvas: one for research, one for consulting, and one for the regions (the bankers). We brought these canvases to the workshop.

All three canvases pointed to the same three competitive advantages over the large consulting groups delivering a similar service:

- Rich data
- Subject matter expertise
- Relevant research

The areas they all agreed were weak were:

- Client engagement methodology
- Reference accounts
- Reputation in this new space

These findings were the foundation for establishing the vision for Global Advisory Services and developing the business strategy for the division:

- The vision: **Grow Big Fast**
- The strategy groupings:
  - ✓ Strategic imperatives
  - ✓ Strategic options
  - ✓ Strategic shifts

All of the groupings above are illustrated in the Grow Big Fast Road Map at the end of this chapter.

Next, and last, we moved into how the team would take Global Advisory Services out into the marketplace. The group selected ten global accounts that would be excellent prospects for strategic engagement and would help Advisory Services establish a reputation. We referred to them as The Targeted Ten. We worked with the team to develop an engagement methodology that built off the strengths of all three groups.

To address the parent company concern, the team created a lead-generation incentive for "The Big House," a term we coined for the parent company.

The work we did on the transformation of this new business unit took place over the course of one year. You will see the time line and key milestones at the bottom of the Grow Big Fast Road Map.

As a result of the collaboration between *fassforward* and this president and his team, everyone in the new business unit was empowered to lead a "bittersweet" change. It paid off. They changed the conversations with each other, their organizations, the parent company, and their customers.

They created a shared worldview and established standards they could all live by. When concerns surfaced, they dealt with them in the president's weekly staff meetings. They won business and learned how to work in a different way.

Bittersweet Change Is the Best Kind of Sweet

Recognizing that "something's gotta change" is always the first step—and that's a step of awareness. That is the beginning of the conversation for change—remember, *leadership lives in the conversation*, both the conversations you have with yourself and the conversations you have with your team.

I've shown you examples from companies you know and shared with you stories from my experience, both personal stories and those that show how my team and I at *fassforward* have been able to empower our clients to grow and transform. Without fail, the impetus for change is born in that "aha" moment of knowing that we need to create something new.

In my experience, you can either actively seek out that

moment or you can have it thrust upon you by circumstances. You can be downsized, like my friend Kathy, or perhaps you wake up one day to realize that another company has created a new business out of your weakness, like Netflix was created out of Blockbuster's weakness—and it can be too late. Or you can look at your business, and your life, and know that change is the way to growth and expansion and actively look for ways to progress and achieve.

I encourage you to read this book as the catalyst for the change you want to see. Don't wait for it to be thrust upon you—I say, *take it on* and be the leader you know you can be!

Conclusion

In this book, I have tried to share with you my deep conviction that conversations matter and that they are at the root of what is wrong in so many areas of business today—and are the key to so much that is right. I want to leave you with a few short words about what you actually get out of focusing on Chocolate Conversations.

There is a tangible difference in companies that communicate well, internally and externally, and you can see it in their *EPS*—earnings per share. Their leaders have the confidence that comes of really knowing what's going on in the organization. Their employees have a clear sense of where they're going, why they do what they do, and how to constructively express their concerns. The company itself is nimble and adaptable, comfortable with the dynamic and changing environment we see today. Their customers feel the company is responsive to their needs and innovative in meeting them. You can see the results clearly in performance. Companies like Apple, like Southwest Airlines, like Facebook, like Verizon Wireless, like Netflix, and like many of the others we've talked about are perfect examples of this. They are relevant, growing, and able to scale. And they've all figured out how worldviews, standards, and concerns work for their leaders, their people, their stockholders, and their customers. None of these companies eat up time and money having Chocolate Conversations.

There's something else you get out of focusing on Chocolate Conversations that is personal to you as a leader. I'd put this in the category of "intangibles that have tangible effect." When you make complete conversations and message discipline a priority for yourself, it has an enormous impact on your personal brand as a leader. You come across to your direct reports, your peers, your CEO, and your board as an insightful person, who is able to make sense out of seeming chaos and get people moving in the right direction just by talking to them. This is a powerful component of your leadership. You, as an individual, build up what is in essence an *emotional bank account*, with all the people who know you. As you interact with people in a way that shows them you are trustworthy, keep your promises, extend courtesies, are clear, seek to understand their positions and so on, you make "deposits" into your bank account. This gives you the standing to lead people through challenging times, because you have earned the ability to do so. If you have been derailed by chocolate conversations, people may think that you break promises they thought they heard, fail to extend courtesies, appear duplicitous or arrogant, or focus on making others understand you first. These are all "withdrawals" from the same account that can sap your strength as a leader.

Your understanding of how your people and your customers see you and your company is a direct link to being relevant and fueling growth. When you really connect with purpose and listen instead of just "tell and sell," people see you as consistent, following through on what you promise, unambiguous, and respectful. This fosters a tangible level of trust that lends great strength to your company, and again, is a reflection on your strength and standing as a leader.

I keep saying that conversations have more power than any of us realize. This is where leadership really happens—in the conversations between corporate leaders and their people, between government heads and their constituents, conversations on the world stage and most recently, the conversation that played out in public between financial institutions and regulators. Were those conversations clear? Did you sense who had a handle on their business and who didn't? Were people's standards considered? Did expectations get met? Are we still hearing concerns from everyone—those directly involved and those observing?

You and I both know that a focused leader can avoid the meltdown and grow his or her business even in difficult economic times. So go for it. Move beyond talking generalities and sharing worldviews. Get down to the standards and uncover the expectations people have. Deal with concerns before they come up. Focus relentlessly on relevance. Don't let Chocolate Conversations be the difference between explosive growth and corporate meltdown. After all, leading Bittersweet change doesn't mean you have to have bittersweet conversations. Why not have rich satisfying ones that transform your business?

Sketchnotes

Thank you
Aaron
Rose

Chapter 1

Death by Chocolate:
Unwrapping Chocolate Conversations

A Chocolate Conversation has three main ingredients

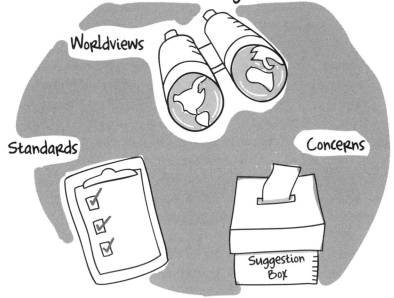

Worldviews

Standards

Concerns

Suggestion Box

To avoid a chocolate conversation and its implications, there are three essentials:

1. Share your worldview

a. Vision is the direction for where you are going
b. Strategy is the map to get there
c. Business model is the system for how you will make money

2. Be clear about your standards

a. Operating model
b. Culture
c. Communication

3. Uncover concerns

a. Anticipate what could go wrong
b. Make the undiscussable, discussable
c. Don't shut people down

Chapter 2:

M&As:
A Petri Dish for Chocolate Conversations

Hanging onto a business model that no longer works is a recipe for slow growth and perpetual cost cutting.

It's important to understand what to let go of—that model, culture, or "sameness" that no longer serves your future.

Many companies do mergers and acquisitions to transform the company. It's a fast way to add what you need.

Most believe it's a $1+1=3$ deal.

Two out of three end with a $1+1\leq1$

Establishing a third identity without diminishing the others is what gets you "1+1=3."

1. Discuss cultural differences and address standards head on.

2. Work together to embrace each other's culture and create the third identity.

3. Appoint an Integration Manager.

Sometimes, companies lose their identity in mergers and their strategic value evaporates right along with it.

A. Porter '13

Chapter 3

Addicted to Relevance

The big question is "are we relevant?" Do customers want what we have? In reality, customers and shareholders will answer that question even if you're not asking it.

Relevance is an idea or product whose time has come.

Relevance is the catalyst for growth

Steve Jobs
was addicted to relevance.

Relevance has always been what makes Apple, Apple. It's the thing about a constantly changing company that has never changed.

You can't turn your company around by borrowing someone else's playbook.

You need to think about how relevance fits into the bigger picture — and translate how it fits into your picture.

Everything to do with leadership and change happens in the conversation, in the context of the Four Considerations of Business.

Relevance	Scale
Growth	Productivity

The only constant we face is change itself

Don't get comfortable, no matter how successful you are. Businesses today can't — and won't — stand still.

Chapter 4

It Starts With You
Leadership happens in the conversation

What we <u>say</u> and what people <u>hear</u> can be very different.

Everyone has to come out of the conversation knowing exactly what's changing, why, and how it will affect them.

Napoleon, a short man with a grand vision, was able to conquer half of Europe.

What set him apart was his ability to convey what was important to them and make it important to others.

Message discipline drives operational discipline.

It's every leader's job to translate.

You have to translate the messages from the top for your employees, so their interpretation is both consistent with the direction of the company and meaningful to them.

What is a Chocolate Conversation
(The Chocolate Conversation Exercise)

They erode confidence, performance, and faith in leadership.

1. Conjure up a picture in your mind when you hear the word chocolate.

2. Ask the question: If a simple concept like "chocolate" can evoke so many interpretations, how does one think something like a company's strategy or change implementation plan will be interpreted by hundreds — or frequently thousands?

A. Porter '13

Chapter 5

Why Do Good People Have Bad Conversations?

The biggest problem arises when people think they have communicated, but the message hasn't made it through.

The gulf widens when what you expect — and what other people think you want — are different.

The key is to see what happens in people's minds as they translate what they think they've heard.

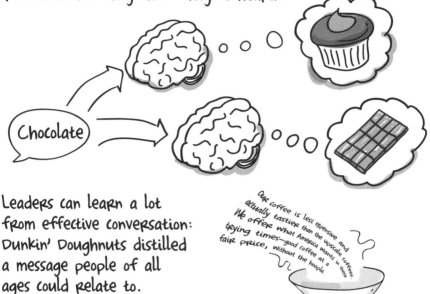

Leaders can learn a lot from effective conversation: Dunkin' Doughnuts distilled a message people of all ages could relate to.

Our coffee is less expensive and actually tastier than the upscale coffees. We offer what America wants in these trying times—good coffee at a fair price, without the hoopla.

Help your people get the picture immediately with simple, clear language.

America Runs on Dunkin'

Remember:

Worldviews shape the picture of reality we carry around in our heads.

Standards are the guidelines we have in our heads that help us know how to act and evaluate what we see.

Concerns arise in our minds based on the way our worldviews and standards influence our perceptions, which inform the way we act.

It's important that people see themselves in the change that has to happen in your company.

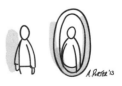

A. Porter '13

Chapter 6:

Go there!

What do people mean when they say, "Don't go there?" It can mean anything from "I don't want to talk about it," to "That's out of bounds."

800-pound
gorilla

Everyone knows
this "gorilla" is sitting there and
yet people do everything they can
to avoid mentioning it.

What people mean when they say "Don't go there" is: there is a background conversation that is off limits, either because it's too scary to be true, or it's too emotional, or — in business — it's politically volatile to bring out into the open.

Leadership happens in the conversation.

Preparing for the hard conversations by providing context reduces the chances for having a chocolate conversation

Deal heat becomes a kind of blindness — a faulty worldview that skews judgment. When the top leadership becomes committed to a new idea, it can push all other considerations out of view.

If you don't go there, your customers will.

Chapter 7

Message Discipline

If you use message discipline effectively, it will translate into operational discipline.

Specific things you can do to bring message discipline to your company.

 What you say: Craft your message carefully — distill it to its essence.

 What gets heard: Listen to your people. Seek feedback and do something with it.

 What gets done: This is the action that is taken as a result of your message.

At the top levels of leadership, it is as important to be a "context expert" as it is to be a content expert. Just think of the difference between the forest and the trees.

People need more context than most leaders provide.

The curse of knowledge: Any time you know significantly more than your audience, you run the risk of assuming they know what you are talking about.

You are your message

Your behaviors have to match your message. If your message is seriously out of sync with the way your people see you, you can do a lot more harm than good.

Chapter 8:

Extending Your Professional Reach

Reaching your people on an emotional level is an indispensable part of your leadership. You can't call yourself a leader if no one is following you.

Emotional intelligence plays a key role in your effectiveness as a leader, your influence on others, and in getting high performance from your teams.

Our areas of greatest strength tend to fall into one of three spheres:

Technical	Social	Political
Professional expertise	Professional network	professional Standing
credibility	influence	power
I earn respect	I marshal resources	I get a seat at the table

Perceptions of others when one sphere is overly relied upon:

Content	Pleasing	Suit
over	over	over
Context	Performing	Substance

The social and political spheres assume an ability to read situations. This is where both message discipline and emotional intelligence come together to complete the package.

It's how you read the gauges and push the buttons

Reading the gauges

Emotional triggers

How people see you

Reading your people

You have to understand where people are coming from.

Pushing the buttons

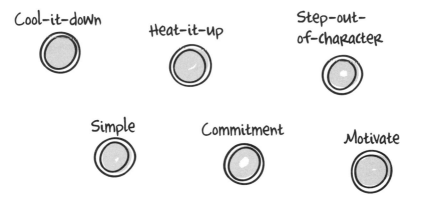

Cool-it-down

Heat-it-up

Step-out-of-character

Simple

Commitment

Motivate

Knowing what to say, how to say it, and when to say it.

A. Porter '13

Chapter 9

Change Is Bittersweet

If you are staying the same
you aren't growing:

o your
business

o your
leadership

o your
people

and you can't TRANSFORM your company.

If you don't identify
the change that's
needed — it will be
thrust upon you.

Change breeds opportunity

Transforming your business may mean you have to rethink
your worldview and establish new standards.

While they are transforming, all businesses must look at the following:

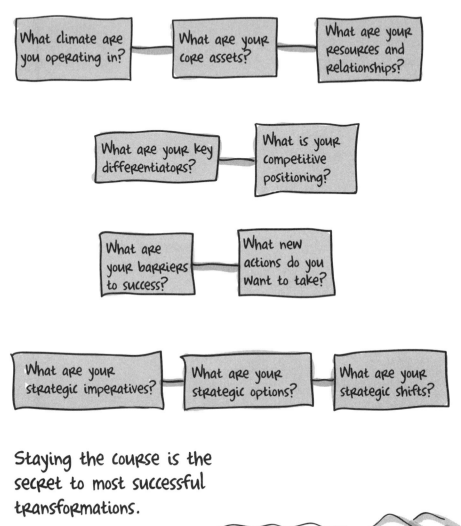

What climate are you operating in?

What are your core assets?

What are your resources and relationships?

What are your key differentiators?

What is your competitive positioning?

What are your barriers to success?

What new actions do you want to take?

What are your strategic imperatives?

What are your strategic options?

What are your strategic shifts?

Staying the course is the secret to most successful transformations.

A. Porter '13

Endnotes

Chapter One

1. Anthony Bianco and Tom Lowry, "Can Dick Parsons Rescue AOL Time Warner?," *Business Week*, May 18, 2003, accessed April 15, 2012, http://www.businessweek.com/stories/2003-05-18/can-dick-parsons-rescue-aol-time-warner.
2. Nina Munk, "Power Failure." *Vanity Fair*, July 2002, accessed April 15, 2012, http://www.ninamunk.com/documents/Power Failure.htm.
3. Claudia Deutsch, "Healing from Executive Trauma," *The New York Times*, March 18, 2001.
4. Louis V. Gerstner, Jr., *Who Says Elephants Can't Dance? Inside IBM's Historic Turnaround* (New York: Harper Business, 2002)
5. David T. Kearns and David A. Nadler, *Prophets in the Dark: How Xerox Reinvented Itself and Beat Back the Japanese* (New York: Harper Collins, 1993)

Chapter Two

1. Michael Bush, "DraftFCB, Two Years After the Merger." *AdAge*, October 13, 2008, accessed April 15, 2012, http://adage.com/article/agency-news/draftfcb-years-merger/131643.

Chapter Three

1. David Kiley, "The New Heat on Ford," *Bloomberg Businessweek Magazine*, June 3, 2007, accessed April 15, 2012, http://www.nbcnews.com/id/18923357/ns/business-us_business/t/new-heat-ford.

2. Alex Salkever, "John, Paul, George, Ringo...and Steve?," *Bloomberg Businessweek Magazine*, September 29, 2004, accessed April 15, 2012, http://www.businessweek.com/stories/2004-09-29/john-paul-george-ringo-dot-dot-dot-and-steve.

3. "Apple Reports First Quarter Results," Apple Press Info, Apple Inc., January 22, 2008, accessed April 15, 2012, http://www.apple.com/pr/library/2008/01/22Apple-Reports-First-Quarter-Results.html.

4. "Apple Becomes World's Most Valuable Brand, Ending Google's Four-Year Term at the Top, says WPP'S BrandZ." *Millward Brown Press Release*, May 8, 2011, accessed June 25, 2012, http://www.millwardbrown.com/Global/News/PressReleases/PressReleaseDetails/11-05-08/Apple_Becomes_World's_Most_Valuable_Brand_Ending_Googles_Four-Year_Term_at_the_Top_says_WPP_S_BrandZ.aspx.

5. Jasper Rees, "The End of Our Kodak Moment," *The Telegraph*, January 19, 2012.

6. Richard Branson, *Losing My Virginity: How I've Survived, Had Fun, and Made a Fortune Doing Business My Way* (New York: Crown Business, 1999),

Chapter Five

1. Bryce G. Hoffman, *American Icon: Alan Mulally and the Fight to Save Ford Motor Company* (New York: Crown Business, 2012), 102.

Chapter Six

1. "Coke Lore: The Real Story of New Coke," The Coca-Cola Company, accessed April 15, 2012, http://www.thecoca-colacompany.com/heritage/cokelore_newcoke.html.

Chapter Seven

1. Bryce G. Hoffman, *American Icon: Alan Mulally and the Fight to Save Ford Motor Company* (New York, Crown Business, 2012), 137–138.

2. Alex Taylor III, "Fixing Up Ford," *Fortune Magazine*, May 11, 2009, accessed June 15, 2012, http://money.cnn.com/2009/05/11/news/companies/mulally_ford.fortune.
3. Alex Taylor III, "Fixing Up Ford," *Fortune Magazine*, May 11, 2009, accessed June 15, 2012, http://money.cnn.com/2009/05/11/news/companies/mulally_ford.fortune.
4. Paul M. Fallon, "Focusing Your Campaign Through Polling and Focus Groups," accessed June 15, 2012, *http://www.completecampaigns.com/article.asp?articleID=9&%20Focus%20Groups.*
5. Paul M. Fallon, "Focusing Your Campaign Through Polling and Focus Groups," accessed June 15, 2012, *http://www.completecampaigns.com/article.asp?articleID=9&%20Focus%20Groups.*

Acknowledgments

So many special people in my career and life contributed to the completion of this book. I doubt anyone writes a book without the support, encouragement, and contribution of others.

I would like to thank Michael Russell who over the past several years patiently worked on this project with me, providing research, editing, and ideas for illustrating concepts and stories. At the beginning of the summer my friend and fellow writer Linda Ruocco joined the project. Linda is one of those people who have a way with words. Thank you for your sage advice, for playing the devil's advocate and for the late nights of editing to get each chapter just right.

I could not have hit all of my deadlines were it not for Maria Zorzos, affectionately known among the *fassforward* team as the *nagarator*, Jess Gozur, and Mary Kinney who just kept plodding along beside her to help me move things along. I also extend my deepest appreciation to the *fassforward* team, who endured many edits and artistic changes, and were a constant sounding board when I was blocked. Thank you Aaron Porter for graphically capturing my words in the illustrative sketchnotes created to conclude the book.

So much of this book was inspired by the work my partner Gavin McMahon and I have done over the past twelve years; thank you Gavin for being an extraordinary partner and friend.

There are those people who work alongside of you for a life time and know just what you need and when you need it. Sally

Zita is that person for me—thank you Sal for always being there.

I thank my dear friend Kevin Allen for introducing me to the publisher, the process, and for being a kindred spirit.

This book would not have been as rich without the contribution of colleagues and clients that took the time out of their busy schedules for interviews and allow me to use our work together in stories throughout the book.

I thank my husband Ron Fass for standing by me for over thirty-five years and for being my biggest fan throughout this process. I also acknowledge our beautiful son, Zachary, for bringing out the best in both of us, thank you Zach for the late night discussions and your candid feedback.

In conclusion, I want to acknowledge Bill McDermott and thank him for writing the Foreword of *The Chocolate Conversation*. Bill encouraged me to write my book. It seemed only fitting that he kick it off... The thing that stands out most in my mind whenever I talk with or about Bill McDermott is the depth of his humanity. Throughout his professional career I have never known him to be too busy to take a phone call or to have a conversation with someone who needed to talk with him. He has always put people first, built great teams, brought out the best in everyone he touches, and over-achieved lofty goals. Bill is a winner and he makes everyone around him a winner too. He gets that personal leadership, market leadership, and real change all happen in the conversation.

Index